Early Literacy

The Editors

Constance Kamii is Professor of Early Childhood Education at the University of Alabama at Birmingham. She studied and conducted research under Jean Piaget as a postdoctoral fellow. Since then she has worked with early childhood educators to help them find ways to use Piaget's constructivist theory in their classrooms.

Maryann and Gary Manning are Professors in the School of Education at the University of Alabama at Birmingham. They are the authors of several NEA publications: *Reading Instruction in the Middle School, Improving Spelling in the Middle Grades,* and *A Guide and Plan for Conducting Reading (K–12) In-Service Workshops.* They are also coauthors of *Reading and Writing in the Primary Grades,* and editors of *Whole Language: Beliefs and Practices, K–8.*

**NEA
EARLY CHILDHOOD
EDUCATION SERIES**

Early Literacy: A Constructivist Foundation for Whole Language

Constance Kamii
Maryann Manning
Gary Manning
Editors

**A NATIONAL EDUCATION ASSOCIATION
P U B L I C A T I O N**

Printing History
    First Printing: September 1991

Note

The opinions expressed in this publication should not be construed as representing the policy or position of the National Education Association. Materials published by the NEA Professional Library are intended to be discussion documents for educators who are concerned with specialized interests of the profession.

Library of Congress Cataloging-in-Publication Data

Early literacy : a constructivist foundation for whole language /
    Constance Kamii, Maryann Manning, Gary Manning, editors
        p.   cm. — (NEA Early childhood education series)
    Includes bibliographical references.
    ISBN 0–8106–0355–1
    1. Language experience approach in education.   2. Constructivism
(Education)   I. Kamii, Constance.   II. Manning, Maryann Murphy.
III. Manning, Gary L.   IV. Series: Early childhood education series
(Washington, D.C.)
LB1576.E18   1991
372.6—dc20   91–19120
                                                                    CIP

CONTENTS

Foreword
by Eleanor Duckworth 7

Introduction
by Constance Kamii, Maryann Manning, and
Gary Manning 9

Chapter 1. What Is Constructivism?
by Constance Kamii 17

Chapter 2. Literacy Acquisition
and the Representation of Language
by Emilia Ferreiro 31

Chapter 3. Principles of Spelling
Found in the First Two Grades
by François Siegrist and Hermina Sinclair 57

Chapter 4. Spelling in Kindergarten:
A Constructivist Analysis Comparing Spanish-
Speaking and English-Speaking Children
by Constance Kamii, Roberta Long,
Maryann Manning, and Gary Manning 69

Chapter 5. Learning to Read in New Zealand
by Brian Cutting and Jerry L. Milligan 83

Chapter 6. Shared Book Experience:
Teaching Reading Using Favorite Books
by Don Holdaway 91

Chapter 7. Modeled Writing: Reflections
on the Constructive Process
by Maryann Manning and Gary Manning 111

Chapter 8. Reading to Know
by Barbara A. Lewis and Roberta Long 119

Chapter 9. An Approach to Assessment
in Early Literacy
by Brenda S. Engel.. 129

Chapter Notes and References.. 149

General References 155

FOREWORD

The basic idea of Piaget's theory as presented in the early chapters of this book—the idea that children construct their own knowledge from the inside rather than internalizing it directly from the outside—can strike a reader as both difficult to grasp and radical. Yet the practice it implies, as described in Chapters 5 and 6 and again in Chapter 9, is highly commonsensical. Why such a curious contradiction?

To those who have watched children as they learn many complex things, those descriptions of classrooms in which all children successfully learn to read have a familiar ring. A *theory* adequate to account for such an enormously complex phenomenon as human learning is, however, another matter. It is not really surprising that many oversimple attempts have been made. Some such attempts that capture small parts of the phenomenon even sound all right, and we start to believe they are adequate across the board. A theory that refuses to oversimplify the nature of human learning then has a double burden: it is not simple to grasp, and it goes counter to very deeply entrenched alternatives.

In our schools, we have come to take for granted a set of practices that are drawn from inadequate theories, and that have little resonance with our ideas about learning in any other setting. This book shows us how an adequate theory can account for practice that is consistent with our commonsense ideas about learning. Don Holdaway points out, for example, that the *work* of figuring out what written marks "say" is joyous for children—an observation wholly consistent with constructivism, but not with conventional theories of how children learn in school. Common sense bolstered by theory makes a powerful support for a practice that is well grounded in both.

The fine thing about a productive theory is that it also takes us *beyond* our current common sense. The work started by

Emilia Ferreiro is full of fascinating revelations of children's understanding of what reading and writing are about. Several chapters of this book afford us glimpses of children's minds at work in wholly surprising ways.

Wary of the potential for the whole-language movement to become an ill-understood fad, vulnerable to distortions of practice, the editors of this book have provided us a sounding board, a testing ground, against which to try our ideas. The book will make an important contribution toward keeping our practice honest.

—Eleanor Duckworth
Professor of Education
Harvard University

INTRODUCTION

The purpose of this book is to consider early literacy education and whole language from the perspective of constructivist theory and research. More specifically, our purposes are (1) to show that the whole-language movement is part of a larger revolution in how we think about learning and teaching and (2) to enable whole-language advocates to explain, evaluate, and improve upon their beliefs and practices on the basis of a scientific, explanatory theory about how children acquire knowledge.

Jean Piaget developed his theory, constructivism, in opposition to another scientific theory, associationism. According to associationism and its better-known outgrowth, behaviorism, knowledge is acquired by *internalizing* certain connections, contingencies, and stimuli from sources external to the individual. By contrast, constructivism states that human beings acquire knowledge by building it *from the inside* in interaction with the environment. For example, as explained further in Chapter 1, many children begin by saying that wind is made by trees (because the branches move when wind is present). Upon being asked how the trees move, young children reply that this movement is caused by wind. Children cannot be said to have acquired this knowledge by internalizing it from the environment.

Constructivism and behaviorism are both scientific theories that have been confirmed all over the world. Two scientific theories can be contradictory and yet true when they are related in the way they are illustrated in Figure 1. This relationship shows that constructivism can explain everything behaviorism can explain but that the converse is not true. Piaget explained conditioning by saying that all animals adapt to their environment. But human beings are more complicated and construct more knowledge than lower animals. Behaviorism can explain conditioning but cannot explain, for example, why children engage in the circular reasoning cited previously. Neither can behaviorism explain why children later become aware of the error in their own reasoning. According to constructivism, children acquire knowledge by creating one level after another of "wrong" forms of knowledge.

As we show in Figure 1, the relationship between behaviorism and constructivism is analogous to the one between the geocentric and heliocentric theories of the universe. The geocentric theory was no longer viewed as true when the heliocentric theory was universally accepted. However, from our limited perspective on earth, it is still true today that the sun rises and sets. This "truth" is reported daily in the news. It is likewise still true, from the limited perspective of surface behavior, that drill and conditioning "work." From a deeper and longer-range perspective, however, we no longer believe that human beings acquire knowledge by internalization, reinforcement, and conditioning.

The whole-language perspective developed independently of constructivism, but the thinking involved is very similar, as can be seen in Chapter 6 by Holdaway. Like constructivists, proponents of whole language rejected the behavioristic conception of reading and writing as a collection of surface skills and bits of information. Educators in mathematics, too, are undergoing a similar revolution away from teaching arithmetic as a set of symbols and rules to be internalized through practice and reinforcement. This change toward constructivism in elementary mathematics can be seen in Clements and Battista (1990), Fosnot (1989), Kamii (1982, 1985, 1989), Labinowicz (1985), Steffe and Cobb (1988), and Yackel, Cobb, Wood, and Merkel (1990). Similar changes are taking place in elementary science education as well (Duckworth, Easley, Hawkins, and Henriques, 1990; Eberhart, Philhower, Sabatino, Smith, and Waterhouse, 1990; Watson and Konicek, 1990).

Figure 1
The Relationships Between Behaviorism and Constructivism
and
Between the Geocentric and Heliocentric Theories

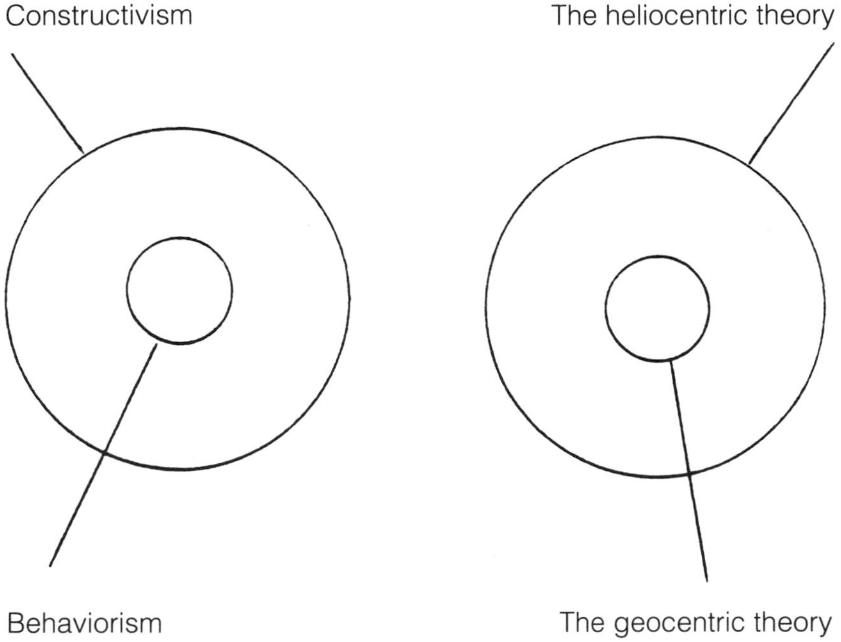

Constructivism   The heliocentric theory

Behaviorism   The geocentric theory

Whole language is defined as a set of beliefs. Altwerger, Edelsky, and Flores (1987) provide the following description:

> First and foremost: Whole Language is *not* practice. It is a set of beliefs, a perspective. It must become practice but it is not the practice itself. Journals, book publishing, literature study, thematic science units and so forth do not make a classroom "Whole Language." Rather, these practices become Whole Language-like because the teacher has particular beliefs and intentions.
>
> Whole Language is based on the following ideas: (a) language is for making meanings, for accomplishing purposes; (b) written language is language—thus what is true for language in general is true for written language; (c) the cuing systems of language (phonology in oral, orthography in written language, morphology, syntax, semantics, pragmatics) are always simultaneously present and interacting in any instance of language in use; (d) language use always occurs in a situation; (e) situations are critical to meaning-making. (p. 145)

Whole language is thus a set of beliefs related to teaching that grew slowly out of many sources such as psycholinguistic research and theory and beliefs about good teaching (Y. Goodman, 1989). By contrast, constructivism is a scientific theory that explains how children and the human species acquire knowledge, without addressing teaching. The explanatory power of a scientific theory enables us to explain, evaluate, and improve upon our practice. In medicine, for example, physicians *know* that the cause(s) of cancer is (are) not known, and that they can therefore treat only the symptoms. In education, by contrast, practitioners often treat only the symptoms (surface behavior) *without knowing* that they are leaving the underlying cause untouched.

Beliefs often contain contradictory elements, and when there is an attack from the outside or a disagreement inside the group, the proponents of the beliefs cannot respond on the basis of a scientific, explanatory theory. The first author of this

Introduction believes that an example of a contradictory element in whole language is the term "cuing systems" found in the preceding quote from Altwerger et al. (1987). A cue is a signal for an actor on stage to do something or to say something. A cue thus comes from outside the individual, but whole-language advocates believe that "cues" originate inside the child.

The preceding example is not a quibble about terminology because the terms we use are manifestations of our thinking. Only when our thinking is logical and tightly linked to scientific evidence and theoretical constructs can we defend our practices with a scientific argument. Furthermore, when a practice becomes popularized and practitioners incorrectly claim to be using Method X, only a scientific, explanatory theory will show that the claim is not justified. An extreme example of a set of beliefs that died is Open Education. When Open Education became popular, it was often thought of as the mere absence of walls separating classrooms. The result was that teachers were left without walls, not knowing what to do. Many people then said that this disaster proved the unsoundness of Open Education!

Such an extreme misunderstanding of beliefs is rare, but the same fate was suffered by other sets of beliefs such as Progressive Education and the Montessori Method. Disagreements developed among their proponents, especially after the death of the respective leaders, and one opinion became as good as another in the absence of a scientific, explanatory theory. The Montessori Method even came to be represented by two separate organizations, the American Montessori Society and the International Montessori Association, both claiming to stand for the true Montessori tradition. Because some skills-oriented books are beginning to be advertised as whole-language books, and some teachers are likewise making incorrect claims, we are concerned about the future of the whole-language movement. We hope this volume will suggest a scientific foundation for whole language including the name. *Whole* is the opposite of *part*. The term "whole language" therefore denotes a mere opposition to language fragmented into parts, but there is much more to whole language than its opposition to cut-up language. It may be, as Jerome Harste stated at the 1990 Whole Language Umbrella Conference, that this term will eventually change. As educators continue to focus on children's constructive process, there will be less need to use a term like "whole language."

The first four chapters of this book begin by describing constructivism and the research supporting it. In Chapter 1 entitled "What Is Constructivism?" Constance Kamii answers this question and gives examples of children's construction of knowledge in meteorology, biology, mechanics, social studies, temporal relationships, and logic. In these examples, she points out that children first make lower-level relationships in all areas of knowledge and go on to make higher-level relationships with the ones they created earlier. A basic tenet of constructivism is thus that children acquire knowledge by constructing one level after another of being "wrong."

In Chapter 2, Emilia Ferreiro summarizes her ground-breaking literacy research with Spanish-speaking young children in Argentina and Mexico. She began her research by reasoning that if young children construct their knowledge of astronomy, meteorology, biology, etc., before going to school, they must surely also have ideas about the written squiggles they see on boxes, street signs, and billboards. Armed with this hypothesis, Ferreiro unearthed surprising rules about reading and writing that children construct at earlier ages than suspected. The difference between a *code* and a *system of representing language* that she explains is a particularly important distinction for educators to understand.

In Chapter 3, François Siegrist and Hermina Sinclair describe a study that extends Ferreiro's research into the first two grades. Siegrist and Sinclair present findings about two principles of spelling that French-speaking children in Geneva construct and subsequently coordinate. The significance of these facts is that children do not all construct social knowledge in the same sequence, but they all construct it by creating their own principles of organization.

Chapter 4 by Constance Kamii, Roberta Long, Maryann Manning, and Gary Manning presents some of the error patterns that a sample of American kindergartners constructed in spelling. Despite the fact that the subjects of the studies discussed in Chapters 2–4 spoke different languages, the constructive process was found to be basically the same. Only minor differences were found across languages.

The rest of the book deals with classroom practices and related issues such as assessment. These practices did not grow out of constructivism but seem to be congruent with it and are used by advocates of whole language. In Chapters 5 and 6 we take the reader to New Zealand, the country with the highest literacy rate in the world. Brian Cutting and Jerry L. Milligan summarize (in Chapter 5) the major differences between New Zealand's national instructional policies and the prevailing methods of teaching in the United States. Since the United States is 49th in literacy among the 159 countries of the world, according to a recent study cited by the authors, the implications suggested by this comparison provide a more convincing argument for the "how to" of literacy instruction than the endless debate involving phonics and whole language.

Chapter 6 by Don Holdaway is entitled "Shared Book Experience: Teaching Reading Using Favorite Books" but deals with much more than "big books." In this chapter Holdaway rejects old pedagogical assumptions and reinforcement theory and traces a new line of investigation that began over 25 years ago in New Zealand focusing on children's "natural, developmental learning" (from within). After all, the author argues, children's learning to walk and talk is self-initiated and self-sustained with deep satisfaction. Very young children manifest their love of books by engaging in reading-like behaviors and pester adults to read the same books again and again. Holdaway's rationale for a new approach to teaching reading exemplifies the same

15

conceptual revolution that Piaget had undergone in Europe.

In Chapter 7 Maryann and Gary Manning analyze modeled writing, a whole-language activity, from a constructivist perspective. An important point they make is that different children learn different aspects of reading and writing during the same activity.

Chapter 8 is different from the others in that Barbara A. Lewis and Roberta Long attempt to explain why children love certain books. After analyzing specific books, the authors conclude that good books correspond to the way children construct knowledge and understanding of human relationships. The relationships among language, thought, and knowledge are not well understood, and we hope this chapter will inspire others to examine how children's books can be written and used to match children's natural desire to know.

The book concludes with a chapter on assessment by Brenda S. Engel. Achievement tests are developed within the framework of behaviorism and associationism. When we move to a constructivist view of literacy development, achievement tests become completely obsolete. Engel shows us how we can assess children's progress within a deeper, broader, longer-range perspective. A particular strength of this chapter is that Engel explains how the same raw data can be used differently, and sometimes quantified, to inform different groups, such as teachers, parents, administrators, and the public.

Educational practices do not flow directly out of constructivism, and it is not possible to conceptualize one "correct" method that can be called "constructivist." As you read this small volume critically, we hope you will join us in our efforts to advance educational practices by basing them on a scientific explanation of how human beings acquire knowledge.

—Constance Kamii
Maryann Manning
Gary Manning

Chapter 1

WHAT IS CONSTRUCTIVISM?

by Constance Kamii, University of Alabama at Birmingham

The author, a former student and postdoctoral research fellow under Jean Piaget, provides an explanation of his theory, constructivism. Focusing on language acquisition first as the most obvious example of the constructive process, she explains that children acquire knowledge by constructing it from the inside, in interaction with the environment, rather than by internalizing it directly from the outside. She goes on to give many other examples to show that children construct their own knowledge of physics, biology, and geography as well as temporal relationships and logic, too, without waiting to be instructed in school.

She concludes by saying that Piaget did not study children's construction of written language, but that this was done by Emilia Ferreiro, the author of Chapter 2.

HOW CHILDREN CONSTRUCT KNOWLEDGE

Jean Piaget is often presented in introductory textbooks and courses only as the theorist who identified stages of cognitive development. This view is unfortunate because, for educators, the significance of Piaget's work lies not in the stages he found but in constructivism, his theory about how human beings

17

acquire knowledge. The stages Piaget found are important only insofar as they support constructivism.

For centuries educators have assumed that children acquire knowledge by *internalizing* it from the environment. Constructivism shows, however, that children acquire knowledge not by internalizing it directly from the outside but by *constructing* it from the inside, in interaction with the environment. Language acquisition is the most obvious example of the constructive process. Since most American children learn to speak English and most French children learn to speak French, it is easy to believe that human beings learn their mother tongue by internalizing it from the environment. A closer look, however, leads us to another conclusion. Babies first utter single "words" such as "Ba-a!" (ball) in spite of the fact that no one in their environment talks in this way. They later say more than one word such as "Ball gone" and "Daddy sock," and go on to produce utterances such as "Markie falled me. Markie me pushed." Still later, they make even more sophisticated errors such as "My foots hurt," and "I thinked it in my head."

Children cannot be said to have learned any of these expressions by direct internalization from the environment because no one in the environment talks in these ways. Young children all over the world learn to talk by constructing one level after another of "wrong" forms of their native speech. This is particularly clear in the way they construct grammatical rules for forming plurals ("my foots") or the past tense ("I thinked"). Children do not learn by internalizing knowledge in ready-made form.

Just as they learn to speak without a single lesson, children construct their own knowledge of physics, astronomy, meteorology, biology, geology, and social institutions before going to school. Piaget (1924/1964, 1926/1967, 1927/1966) asked children questions about the nature of air; the origin of wind, breath, the sun and the moon, stones, trees, rivers, mountains, and the earth; how clouds move; why boats float;

how bicycles work; what families and countries are, etc. A few examples of their answers will help explain how children construct knowledge.

Wind. With respect to the nature of wind, Piaget (1927/1966) asked: "Where does the wind come from? . . . There is (or there is not) a lot of wind to-day. There was (or there was not) a lot of wind yesterday. Why is that? . . . (and) How did the wind begin? . . . The first time there was any wind, where did it come from?" (p. 33). He grouped the answers children gave into three levels. The characteristics of the first level, found mostly around age 5, were artificialism and finalism: Wind is produced by man or God, or by means of breath or machines, and is *made for* rain, trees, boats, etc. During the second stage, at 8 years of age on average, children said that wind was made by clouds, trees, waves, dust, etc. By age 10, in contrast, they stated that wind made itself from air but were unable to explain how this happened. Below is an example of an interview with an 8-year-old at level 2:

> Grat (8): "Where does the wind come from?—*From the trees.*—How did the wind begin?—*Because the branches move.*—Do the branches make the wind?—*Yes.*—But how do the branches move?—*Because of the wind.*" (p. 40)

As can be seen above, children construct theories or hypotheses about objects and phenomena by putting things into relationships. When they put previously made relationships into relationship (trees cause wind, and the wind makes trees move) and become aware of their circular reasoning, they go on to construct a more adequate explanation.

Breath. Closely related to wind is the biological phenomenon of breathing. Piaget (1927/1966) asked children to blow on their hand and asked a number of questions in the following interview:

> Mon (7): ". . . What happens when you blow?—*Air.*—Where does it come from?—*From outside.* [Naturally, Mon, like all the

19

children, assumes that there's no air in the room. Besides which, the window is shut.]—Is there air in the room?—*No.*—In your mouth?—*Yes.*—Where does it come from?—*From out-side.*—How did it come?—. . .—How did it get inside you?—*Through the mouth.*" "Is there air in your mouth just now?—*No.*—Blow! Where does that air come from?—*From outside.*" (p. 54)

Mon is an example of level 1, when "wind is regarded as having a double origin—internal, because we make air, and external, because we attract the air from outside or the wind . . . comes and settles itself in us" (pp. 52–53). At the second level, the child says that air is all around us and that we breathe the air that is in the room. However, if there were no air in the room, we would make some by breathing! In the third stage, the child's ideas become like ours.

The action of blowing is observable, but air is not. The invisibility of air, however, is not the reason why, in stage 1, children say that breath can come from the air outside even when there is no air in the room. The following example from Piaget's research on children's knowledge of bicycles illustrates how children do not put things into precise relationships, even when all the parts are observable.

Bicycles. Every boy was familiar with bicycles in the 1920s. Piaget (1927/1966) describes the questions he put to children in the following way:

We say to the child: "Do you like looking at bicycles in the street? Very well then, draw me a bicycle on this piece of paper." The boy will often protest: "But I can't draw," etc. But we insist. "Do it as well as you can. I know it is difficult, but go ahead, your friends can do it and you'll be able to too." Care should be taken not to let the drawing be too small (7 centimetres at least). If necessary, one can outline the two wheels for the youngest children (it is a question of explana-tion not of drawing!) and wait for them to finish the rest. Then we ask: "Well, and how does a bicycle go?" If the child answers "With wheels," we go on, "yes, but how, what happens when the gentleman sits there?" .... Finally, ... we point to the parts that have been drawn, the pedals, the chain, the cog-wheels, and ask about each in turn: "What is that for?" (pp. 197–198)

Figure 1.1, which is adapted from the original, shows in (d) an example of a drawing considered complete. It has (1) two wheels, (2) one cog-wheel between the two wheels, (3) another cog-wheel in the center of the back wheel, (4) a chain connecting the two cog-wheels, and (5) the pedals fixed to the large cog-wheel.

At 4–5 years of age, during the first of the four stages Piaget found, the cause of movement was conceived vaguely and globally. The child said, for example, that it was "the mechanism" that made the bicycle go. As can be seen in Figure 1.1(a), the child thought only about a few elements of the bicycle (two wheels and a pedal) and did not put them into a relationship.

During the second stage, at 5 to 6 years of age, the elements became more numerous and precise as illustrated in Figure 1.1(b). But the cause of the movement was still global. Below is an example of children's vague reasoning:

Al (6): The bicycle goes with the wheels and *"the gentleman makes them work.—How?—When he's riding. He pedals with his feet. That makes the wheels work.*—What is the chain for?—*To hold the wheels, no, the pedals. The handle-bar makes the wheels and the pedals go.*—What is the chain for?—*To hold the pedals.*—And the pedals?—*To make the wheels go.*—And the wheels?—*To make the bicycle go.*" (p. 207)

At stage 3, the action of each element became clearer, but the child could not put all the elements into a single, simultaneous system of relationships.

Dher (8;1) at age eight years and one month said, for example: "*The gentleman makes the pedals turn. The wheels turn*

21

Figure 1.1
Children's Drawings of a Bicycle

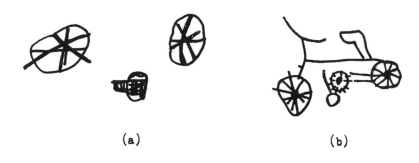

(a)

(b)

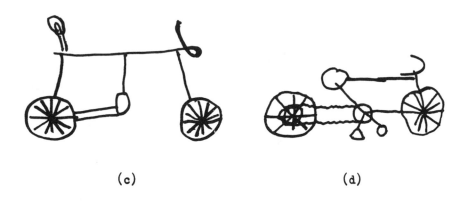

(c)

(d)

Adapted from *The Child's Conception of Physical Causality,* by Jean Piaget (Paterson, N.J.: Littlefield, Adams, 1966).

with them. There is a chain that is joined to the pedals and the wheels" (p. 211). As shown in Figure 1.1(c), the chain may be connected to a tire and to a pedal at this stage.

At approximately age 8, however, most boys put all the elements into a single system of relationships. The protocol of In (8;3) and Figure 1.1(d) illustrate this system: *"You pedal and it makes a wheel* [the cog-wheel] *go round. There's a chain, and it makes the back wheel go round"* (p. 211).

The examples given so far belong to what Piaget called physical knowledge, i.e., knowledge of objects. Let us go on to an example of social knowledge, the kind of knowledge that has its sources in conventions made by people.

A town and country. Piaget (1924/1964, 1951/1976) asked children about the relationship between Switzerland and Geneva. Below is the example of Claude (6;9), a child at level 1 who answered questions and was then asked to draw circles to show the spatial relationship between Geneva and Switzerland:

What is Switzerland? *It's a country.* And Geneva? *A town.* Where is Geneva? *In Switzerland* (The child draws the two circles side by side but the circle for Geneva is smaller). *I'm drawing the circle for Geneva smaller because Geneva is smaller. Switzerland is very big.* Quite right, but where is Geneva? *In Switzerland.* Are you Swiss? *Yes.* And are you Genevese? *Oh no! I'm Swiss now.* (Piaget, 1976/1951, p. 40)

Children at the next level (at 7–8 to 10–11 years of age) drew Geneva inside Switzerland but continued to insist that they could not be both Swiss and Genevan at the same time. When they made the correct part-whole relationship both spatially and logically, the children were categorized in level 3.

Age differences. In *The Child's Conception of Time,* Piaget (1946/1971) reports findings from his interviews about age differences. Below is an example from his interview with Rom, a four-year-old who had a younger sister named Erica:

Who is the older of you two? *Me.* Why? *Because I'm the bigger*

23

one. Who will be older when she starts going to school? *Don't know.* When you are grown up, will one of you be older than the other? . . . *Don't know.* Is your mother older than you? *Yes.* Is your Granny older than your mother? *No.* Are they the same age? *I think so.* Isn't she older than your mother? *Oh no.* Does your Granny grow older every year? *She stays the same.* And your mother? *She stays the same as well.* And you? *No, I get older.* And your little sister? *Yes!* (categorically). (p. 221)

Note that Rom's answers about age differences are all based on people's sizes. She says that she is older than her younger sister "because I'm the bigger one" and does not know if she will still be older when Erica goes to school or when both grow up. Since her mother and grandmother are about the same height and do not grow taller, Rom believes that they are the same age and do not grow older. When Rom constructs a system of temporal relationships, she will become able to deduce age differences from this temporal framework (which will be explained shortly).

Class inclusion. In the class-inclusion task (Inhelder and Piaget, 1964/1959), the child is presented, for example, with six miniature dogs and two cats of the same size and is asked, "What do you see?" so that the examiner can proceed with words from the child's vocabulary. The child is then asked to show "all the animals," "all the dogs," and "all the cats" with words such as "doggies" that the child used. Only after ascertaining the child's understanding of these terms does the adult ask the following class-inclusion question: "Are there more dogs or more animals?"

Four-year-olds typically answer, "More dogs," where-upon the adult asks, "Than what?" The four-year-olds' answer is: "Than cats." In other words, the question the examiner asks is "Are there more dogs or more animals?" but the one young children "hear" is "Are there more dogs or more cats?" Young children hear a question that is different from the one the adult asks because once they have mentally cut the whole (animals) into two parts (dogs and cats), the only thing they can think about is the two parts (dogs and cats). For them, at that moment,

24

the whole no longer exists. They can think about the whole, but not when they are thinking about the parts. In order to compare the whole with a part, the child has to perform two opposite mental actions at the same time—cut the whole into two parts and put the parts back together into a whole. This, according to Piaget, is precisely what four-year-olds cannot do.

By eight years of age, Piaget states, most children's thought becomes mobile enough to be reversible. Reversibility refers to the ability to mentally perform opposite actions *simultaneously*—in this case, to separate the whole into two parts and reunite the parts into a whole. In physical, material action, it is not possible to do two opposite things simultaneously. In our heads, however, this is possible, when thought has become mobile enough to be reversible. It is only when the parts can be reunited in the mind that a child can "see" that there are more animals than dogs.

The preceding discussion about children's construction of knowledge treated each example as if it were an independent construction. I now turn to the distinction Piaget made between knowledge in a narrow sense and knowledge in a broad sense to show that children construct knowledge as an organized whole.

KNOWLEDGE IN A NARROW SENSE AND KNOWLEDGE IN A BROAD SENSE

Knowledge in a narrow sense is easy to understand. It refers to specific bits of information such as the fact that Washington is the capital of the United States (Furth 1969). To understand what a capital and "the United States" are, however, we need a classificatory framework. We also need a spatial framework that enables us to locate the United States in space and to make the part-whole relationship between a city and a country. Knowledge in a broad sense refers to these and other systems of relationships that enable us to organize our knowledge and to interpret new information.

If we tried to teach preschool children that Washington is the capital of the United States, the most we would get would be rote recitation. The children would not understand the statement because they do not have the general framework of knowledge into which they need to fit the statement in order to understand it. Even the four-year-olds living in Washington, D.C., would not understand that they live in a city and a country *at the same time*. To them "capital" may mean a person, a building, or nothing at all.

A third grader can more or less understand that Washington is the capital of the United States. However, knowing the relationship between London and England, Paris and France, and a state and a state capital will help this child better understand the relationship between Washington and the United States. Studying history and civics and fitting current events about the president of the United States, the mayor of Washington, D.C., and various senators will further help the child elaborate his knowledge about Washington, D.C., in a broad sense.

Piaget distinguished three kinds of knowledge according to their ultimate sources and modes of structuring: physical, logico-mathematical, and social (conventional) knowledge. These are discussed below to clarify the nature of knowledge in a broad sense and in a narrow sense.

Three Kinds of Knowledge

Physical knowledge is knowledge of objects in external reality. The color, weight, and shape of a dog are examples of physical properties that are *in* objects in external reality that can be known empirically by observation.

Logico-mathematical knowledge, on the other hand, consists of the relationships created by each individual. For instance, when we see a dog and a cat and think that they are *different*, this difference is an example of a relationship, which belongs to logico-mathematical knowledge. The dog and the cat are observable, but the difference between them is not. The difference exists neither *in* the dog nor *in* the cat, and if a person did not put the objects into this relationship, the difference would not exist for him or her. Other examples of relationships the individual can create between the dog and the cat are *similar* and *two*. The source of logico-mathematical knowledge is thus in the head of each individual who puts objects and events into relationships.

The ultimate sources of social knowledge are conventions made by people. Examples of social knowledge are the fact that Christmas comes on December 25, that a dog is called "dog"in English, and that "dog" is written in a certain way.

Logico-mathematical knowledge, the most complicated of the three kinds of knowledge, would take too long to explain adequately here. Suffice it to say that a part of logico-mathematical knowledge is the logico-mathematical framework through which we organize the totality of our knowledge. Another way of making the same statement is to say that there can be no physical or social (conventional) knowledge without a logico-mathematical framework. For example, we would not be able to recognize a dog as a dog if we did not have a classificatory framework that enables us to think about "dogs"as opposed to other animals, and "animals"as opposed to other objects.

The logico-mathematical framework includes a classifica- tory organization and a spatio-temporal organization. We have already examined the classificatory framework necessary to understand the words "capital" and "the United States." To locate the United States and Washington, D.C., in space, however, we need a spatial framework. In addition, we need a temporal framework to locate George Washington, Abraham Lincoln, and those who died in the Vietnam War in time as we visit the memorials erected to honor these individuals.

The logico-mathematical framework is constructed by each child, over many years, by making relationships and coordinating these relationships. In the class-inclusion task, we have seen how young children can make categories such as "dogs," "cats," and "animals" but cannot put these categories into a single, simultaneous, hierarchical structure until their thought becomes mobile enough to be reversible. We saw in the interview about Geneva and Switzerland that spatial relationships, too, must be constructed gradually by each child. Knowing that one is living in Geneva and Switzerland at the same time involves a spatial relationship, but knowing that one can be a Genevan and a Swiss at the same time involves a classificatory relationship that is dependent on the child's construction of the spatial relationship between Geneva and Switzerland. While time is irrelevant to these spatial and classificatory relationships, it is all-important in knowing age differences. Until children have constructed a system of temporal relationships, they are not able to deduce that age differences among individuals are constant. The interviews about wind, breath, and bicycles concerned physical knowledge. The limited relationships children were making in these interviews illustrate the indispensability of logico-mathematical knowledge for the construction of physical knowledge. Young children did not feel anything was wrong in saying that trees cause wind, and that the wind makes trees move. Likewise, they did not see anything wrong about saying that there is no air in the room and that their breath came from the outside. The bicycles they drew explicitly demonstrated the fact that even physical knowledge is not mere empirical knowledge.

Knowledge in the broad sense is thus organized within a logico-mathematical framework, which each child must spend many years to construct. While this knowledge cannot simply be given or transmitted to the child, adults can do many things to hamper or facilitate the child's possibility of constructing knowledge. For example, a child who has the possibility of hearing English is more likely to construct the English language than one who is not exposed to English. Likewise, a child who has traveled abroad is more likely to construct the meaning of "the United States" than one who has never been outside his or her neighborhood.

Young Children's Knowledge of Written Language

Piaget did not study children's conception of reading and writing, but this was undertaken by one of his collaborators, Emilia Ferreiro (Ferreiro and Teberosky 1979/1982). She hypothesized on the basis of Piaget's theory that if children construct their own knowledge of the sun, the moon, trees, rivers, mountains, clouds, wind, bicycles, countries, etc., they must surely also have ideas about the written squiggles they see all around them—on boxes, bottles, street signs, machines, store windows, etc. The child in Piaget's theory is not a passive recipient who waits to be instructed in school. For Piaget, children are producers of knowledge who try to make sense of everything they encounter in their environment.

Ferreiro's findings are presented in her own words in the next chapter. The only thing I would like to point out in concluding this chapter is that Ferreiro studied children's conception of written language as cultural objects to be known, and not merely as tools to be used or skills to be learned. To try to make sense of these cultural objects, young children busily use the knowledge in a broad sense that they have been constructing since the day they were born.

Chapter 2

LITERACY ACQUISITION AND THE REPRESENTATION OF LANGUAGE

by Emilia Ferreiro, Center of Research and Advanced Studies, National Polytechnic Institute, Mexico City

In this chapter, Ferreiro offers yet another ground-breaking idea: The writing system is a representation of language *rather than a* code. *She points out that "the invention of a writing system was the outcome of a historical process during which a system of representation, not a code, was constructed."*

Children must reconstruct the system of representation, if they are to become readers and writers. If you agree with Ferreiro, the implications for the teaching of reading and writing will become clear. The writing system cannot be taught merely as "a code of transcription that converts sound into graphic entities."

If you are not already familiar with Ferreiro's work, we recommend the fascinating book she co-authored with Ana Teberosky, Literacy Before Schooling *(1979/1982).*

To the reader unfamiliar with Ferdinand de Saussure's work (1915/1966), the terms "linguistic symbol," "signifier," "signified," and "referent" may be confusing. When Ferreiro speaks of "linguistic symbols" in this chapter, she is referring to spoken words, such as "tree." For Saussure, this spoken word is a union of a concept and a sound-image (which are both psychological, i.e., inside the individual). As can be seen in the figure below, the word "tree" has two sides for Saussure: the concept "tree" and the sound-image "tree." The referent is the tree in the external world. To emphasize the opposition between the concept and the sound-image, Saussure spoke of the signified and the signifier. This distinction helps to understand whether written words represent only sounds or sounds in relation to meaning.

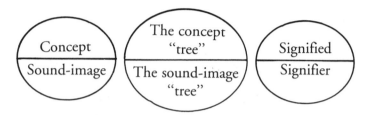

This chapter was originally published in Brazil under the title "A representação da linguagem e o processo de alfabetização," in Cadernos de Pesquisa, *No. 52 (1985): 7–17. Some adaptations were made by the author for this English version.*

Only recently has it become acknowledged that the improvement of literacy acquisition during childhood is the key element for the prevention of illiteracy among adolescents and adults.

Traditional approaches to child literacy acquisition have focused either on the method employed by teachers or on the "maturity" or "readiness" of children. The two poles of the educational process, namely, the one who teaches and the one who learns, have been characterized without taking into account the third element in this relationship: the nature of the object of knowledge involved in this process of learning. I shall attempt to demonstrate how this object of knowledge intervenes in this process not as an independent entity but as part of a triad. The triad consists of the alphabetical representation of language,[1] which has its own peculiar features, and the conceptualization of this object by the learners (children) and by the teachers.

THE WRITTEN MARKS AS A SYSTEM OF REPRESENTATION

The writing system may be conceptualized in two very different ways. The pedagogic consequences of each conceptualization are quite different. The writing system may be conceived as a *representation* of language or as a *code* that allows a graphic transcription of the sound units. These differences need explanation.

The construction of any system of representation involves a process of differentiation among the recognizable properties and relationships in the object to be represented and a selection of those properties and relationships that are to be kept in the representation. A representation "X" is not identical to the piece of "R" (reality) that it represents. (If it were, it would not be a representation but another "R.") Therefore, if a system "X" is to represent a given piece of "R" properly, it should combine two apparently contradictory conditions:

   a. "X" should retain some of the characteristic properties and relationships of "R."
   b. "X" should exclude some of the characteristic properties and relationships of "R."

The relationship between "X" and "R" may be analogic or absolutely arbitrary. For example, if the properties of "R" are forms, distances, and colors, "X" may preserve them and represent forms by forms, distances by distances, and colors by colors. This is what happens in contemporary mapmaking: The coast of a country is not a line, but the line on the map representing it respects the proximity between two points on the

33

coast; differences in altitude do not correspond always to different coloring in "R," but they are generally indicated by different colors in "X," and so on. Although a map is basically an analogic system of representation, it is also arbitrary in some respects. Political boundaries may be indicated by a series of dots, by a continuous line, or by some other device. Cities are never circles or squares and yet these geometrical forms are usually used to represent cities.[2]

The problem of constructing an appropriate system "X" to represent "R" is completely different from that of constructing alternative systems of representation (X1, X2, . . . Xn) based on the original "X." We shall use the term to *code* for the procedure of constructing such alternative systems. Examples of these alternative systems are the transcription of the letters of the alphabet into a telegraphic code, the transcription of digits into a computer binary code, the design of secret codes for military use, and so on. All of these are based on a representation already in use (the alphabetical system for natural language, or the ideographic system for numbers).

The essential difference between these two ways of constructing systems is that *in the case of coding, the properties as well as the relationships are predetermined.* The new code is merely another representation of the same properties and relationships. On the other hand, *in the case of the creation of a system of representation, neither the properties nor the relationships are predetermined.* For example, when the alphabet is transcribed into the Morse code, all the graphic symbols that stand for letters are translated as strings of dots and dashes, and each letter in the first system is represented by a different string of dots and dashes in a one-to-one correspondence. No "new letters" are invented and none are omitted. The construction of a first form of representation is quite another thing. As a rule, it is the outcome of a long historical process that reached its final form by social consensus.

The invention of a writing system was the outcome of a

historical process during which a system of representation, not a new code, was constructed. We might be tempted to think that once the system was constructed, it would be learned by its new users as a code. The actual situation is quite different. In the case of the two basic systems that children must acquire at the beginning of schooling (the representation of numbers and the written representation of language), children face conceptual difficulties similar to those that were encountered during the process of constructing the system. It is for this reason that we may say that children reinvent these two systems. This does not mean that children literally have to reinvent letters and numbers, but it does mean that they must understand the construction process involved in each system and its rules of production (in fact, to reconstruct it) in order to become able to use these letters and numbers as elements of a system. This poses a fundamental epistemological problem: What is the nature of the relationship between reality and its representation?

As regards written language, the complexity of linguistic symbols makes it difficult to select those parameters that are to be privileged in the representation. Starting with the well-known work of Ferdinand de Saussure (1915/1966), we have conceived the linguistic symbol as a single two-sided entity composed of signifier and signified, but we have not fully appreciated its implications for the construction of writing as a system of representation. It is the two-sided nature of the linguistic symbol, the complexity of the symbol itself and of its referentiality, that is the issue at stake. In this respect, we might well ask what the writing system really represents. Does it represent differences in the signifieds, or differences in the signifieds in relation to the properties of the referents? Or does it represent differences among signifiers, or differences among signifiers in relation to the signifieds?

It would appear that alphabetical (as well as syllabic) writing systems might be characterized as systems whose primary or principal aim is to represent differences among signifiers. On

the other hand, ideographic writing systems might be characterized as systems whose primary or principal aim is to represent
differences among the signifieds. Despite this, it could also be
asserted that no writing system has ever succeeded in giving a
balanced representation of the two-sided entity known as the
linguistic symbol. Even though some of them (such as the
alphabetical system) give preference to differences among
signifiers and others (such as the ideographic systems) give
preference to the representation of differences in the signifieds,
not one of them is "pure." Alphabetical systems incorporate
ideographic devices through their orthography (Blanche-Benveniste and Chervel 1974); ideographic (or logographic) systems
likewise incorporate phonetic devices (Cohen 1958; Gelb 1982).
The distinction that we are making between codes and systems of
representation is not merely terminological. Its pedagogical
consequences mark a neat dividing line. If the writing system is
conceived as a code of transcription that converts sound units
into graphic entities, perceptual discrimination in the two
modalities involved (visual and auditory) takes priority. The
reading and writing programs based on this conception
concentrate first of all on exercising these discriminations
without ever questioning the nature of the units used. In this
approach, language is, to a certain extent, placed "in parenthe-
ses" or reduced to a series of sounds (contrasting sounds on the
plane of the signifier). The problem is that once the sound
sequence (the signifier) is divorced from the signified, the
linguistic symbol as such collapses. The supposition behind those
kinds of procedures is almost transparent: If the learner
experiences little or no difficulty in distinguishing one similar
visual form from another, one auditory form from another, and
can also draw them, s/he should have no difficulty starting to read
since s/he simply has to transcribe the auditory to the visual code.

On the other hand, if the acquisition of written language
is conceived as the understanding of the way in which a system of
representation is constructed, the problem may be posed quite

differently. The learner may have a good command of the spoken language and may be able to make all the necessary perceptual discriminations, but this will not solve the central problem, which is to understand the nature of this system of representation. This includes, for example, understanding why some of the fundamental communicative properties of spoken language (such as intonation) are not kept in the representation; why all the words are treated equally in the representation, even though they belong to different "classes"; why similarities in the signified are dismissed in favor of similarities in sound; why differences are introduced into the representation despite conceptual similarities; and so forth.

The final consequence of this dichotomy may be expressed in even more dramatic terms. If the writing system is regarded as a code of transcription, the learning process becomes equated with the acquisition of a technique. However, if it is regarded as a system of representation, the learning process becomes conceived as the acquisition of a new object of knowledge, that is to say, it becomes a conceptual learning process.

CHILDREN'S CONCEPTUALIZATIONS OF THE WRITING SYSTEM

Children's spontaneous productions are the clearest signs of their attempts to understand the nature of the writing system.[3] When a child writes as s/he believes a certain set of words should be written,[4] s/he is offering the most valuable document which should be interpreted in order to be assessed. His/her writing endeavors are often unfairly dismissed as scribbling, "nothing but a game," or the outcome of pretending to write. Learning to read those spontaneous children's productions, that is, to interpret them, takes a long time and requires a sound theoretical attitude. If we believe that children learn only when they are receiving systematic instruction and that they are bound to be ignorant up

37

to this point, we would be unable to see anything in their productions. However, if we consider children as thinking subjects to whom the idea of asking permission to begin learning has not occurred, we might be able to accept that they may have some knowledge even though they have no "institutional authorization" to obtain it. "To know" means having been able to construct some conceptualization that accounts for a certain set of objects or phenomena within a given context of reality. Whether this "knowing" coincides with the socially accepted knowledge is another problem (even though this is precisely what schools consider to be *the* problem of "knowing"). One child may know the name of letters (or conventional spelling) without understanding very much about the writing system. Conversely, another child may make substantial progress in understanding the system as such without ever having received any information about spelling.

At this point, I shall briefly mention some of the aspects that are central to this psychogenetic development, which have been presented and discussed in greater depth in other publications (Ferreiro and Teberosky 1979/1982; Ferreiro 1984a, 1985, 1986).

Children's first writing attempts take various forms, such as broken or continuous wavy lines or zigzags (see Figure 2.1a), or a series of repeated discrete elements (such as vertical lines or circles). The appearance of these forms does not guarantee that the child is in fact writing unless we can establish what the conditions of production are (see Figure 2.1b).[5] The traditional way of examining these first writing attempts consists of focusing on the graphic aspects of the productions and ignoring their constructive aspects. The *graphic aspects* include the quality of the drawing, the spatial distribution of the forms, the predominant orientation (from left to right, from top to bottom), and the orientation of the individual characters (inversions, rotations, etc.). The *constructive aspects* include what the child wanted to represent and the means s/he uses to introduce differentiations.

Figure 2.1a
Example of Writing
Without Interfigural
Differentiation Devices
(Adriana, 4 years, 5 months)

Figure 2.1b
Example of Writing with
Conventional Letters but Without
Intrafigural Differentiation Devices
(Domingo, 6-years-old)

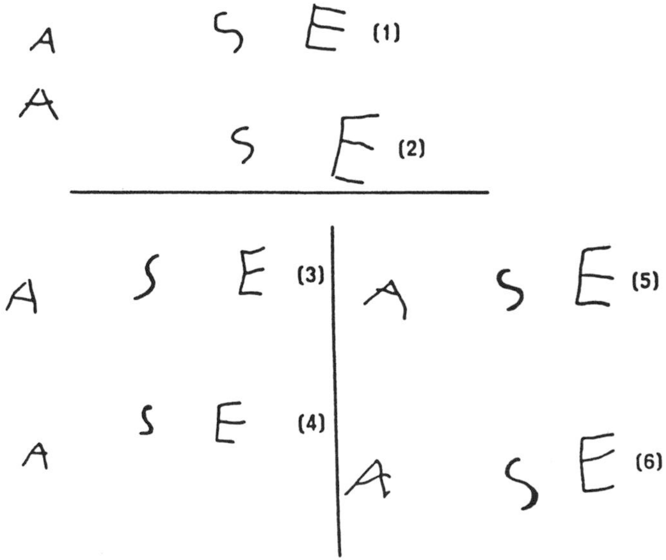

As far as the constructive aspects are concerned, children's first writing attempts run along surprisingly regular developmental lines, despite differences in culture, educational settings and language. There are three major periods, each of which with numerous subdivisions:

- The distinction between the iconic mode of representation and the non-iconic mode of representation

- The elaboration of devices of differentiation (progressive control of variations on the qualitative and quantitative axes)

- The phonetization of writing (beginning with a syllabic period and ending with the alphabetical period)

During the first period, children acquire the two basic distinctions on which they will base the subsequent constructions: the differentiation between the figurative graphic marks and the non-figurative graphic marks, and the constitution of writing as a substitute object.[6] The distinction between "drawing" and "writing" is extremely important (whatever terms are used by children to refer to each activity). When drawing, children are in the domain of the iconic: The graphic forms are important because they reproduce the form of the objects. When writing, they leave this domain. The graphic forms no longer reproduce the form of the objects, nor does their spatial organization reproduce the contour of the same. It is for this reason that both the arbitrariness of the forms chosen and their linear organization are the salient characteristics of preschool writing. Arbitrariness does not necessarily imply conventionality, though conventional forms often do appear at a very early age (see Figure 2.1b). Children do not waste their intellectual efforts on inventing new letters; they take the form of each letter from society and adopt it.

They do, however, put much intellectual effort into constructing ways of differentiating among strings of letters. This is the main characteristic of the next period that has two steps. The criteria of differentiation are first *intrafigural,* and consist of establishing the properties that a written text should have in order that it may be interpreted (that is, in order that it may be given a meaning). On the quantitative axis, these intrafigural criteria consist of a minimum number of letters—generally three—that a text should have if it is "to say something." On the qualitative axis, they consist of the internal variation needed to interpret a string of graphic forms (if the text "always contains the same" letter, it cannot be read or interpreted).[7]

The next step is characterized by the search for objective ways of differentiating one string of letters from another in order to "say something different" (see Figure 2.2). It is at this point that a sophisticated search start for modes of differentiation that are *interfigural.* The conditions of intrafigural legibility are maintained, but new systematic modes of differentiation between one string of letters and another are now created in order to ensure differences in meaning. Children explore criteria that may lead to variations on the quantitative axis (such as varying the quantity of letters in each string of letters in order to obtain different texts) and on the qualitative axis (such as varying the letters in each string of letters or changing the position of the same letters without altering the quantity). The coordination of both modes of differentiation (quantitative and qualitative) is as difficult here as in any other area of cognitive development.

What children write during these first two periods is not ruled by differences or similarities among signifiers (see Figure 2.2). When they start to take into account the similarities or differences in the sounds of signifiers, they enter the third period. Children begin by discovering that the written components of a string (the letters) may correspond to so many parts of the spoken word (its syllables). On the quantitative axis, this leads to the discovery that the amount of letters needed to write a word can

Figure 2.2
Examples of Writing with Intrafigural Differentiations
(Carmelo, 6 years, 2 months)

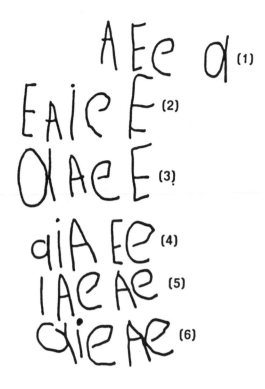

be put in correspondence with the number of parts identifiable when it is spoken. These "parts" of the word are, in the first instance, its syllables. The syllabic period gradually reaches a point of rigorous self-consistence: one syllable per letter, no syllable should be omitted or repeated. This syllabic hypothesis is of the greatest importance for two reasons. First, it allows the child to use a general criterion for regulating the variations in the quantity of letters that should be written, and second, it focuses his/her attention on the differences in the sound pattern of each word (see Figures 2.3a and 2.3b).

The syllabic hypothesis does, however, have its own inherent contradictions. There is a contradiction between the syllabic control and the minimum number of letters that a written noun should contain to be "interpretable" (for example, a monosyllabic word should be written with only one letter, but if only one letter is written down, it "cannot be read," that is to say, it cannot be interpreted). There is also a contradiction between the syllabic interpretation and standard written texts produced by adults (which will *always* contain more letters than the syllabic hypothesis predicts).[8]

In the same period, though not necessarily at the same time, the letters may begin to acquire relatively stable syllabic sound values. This allows the learner to determine new relationships on the qualitative axis: Similar sounding parts of different words start to share similar letters. And this also creates its own peculiar conflicts.

All these conflicts (to which we need to add the influence of schooling depending on the age of the child at this moment) gradually destabilize the syllabic hypothesis until children have enough courage to engage in a new process of construction.[9] The syllabic-alphabetic period marks the transition from the prior schemes they are about to abandon and the future schemes they are about to construct (see Figure 2.4). When they discover that the syllable is not *the* unit but that it may be in turn analyzed in smaller elements, they take the final step toward the comprehension of the socially established system. And, from there on, they discover new problems. On the quantitative axis, they realize that even though one letter need not necessarily stand for one syllable, they cannot establish any kind of rule by duplicating the amount of letters per syllable (since there are syllables that are written with one, two, three or more letters). On the qualitative axis, they have to come to terms with the spelling problems that also lack regularity (similarity of sounds does not ensure similarity of letters or vice versa).

Figure 2.3a	Figure 2.3b
Example of Syllabic Writing	Example of Syllabic Writing
(Jorge, 6-years-old)	(Francisco, 6-years-old)

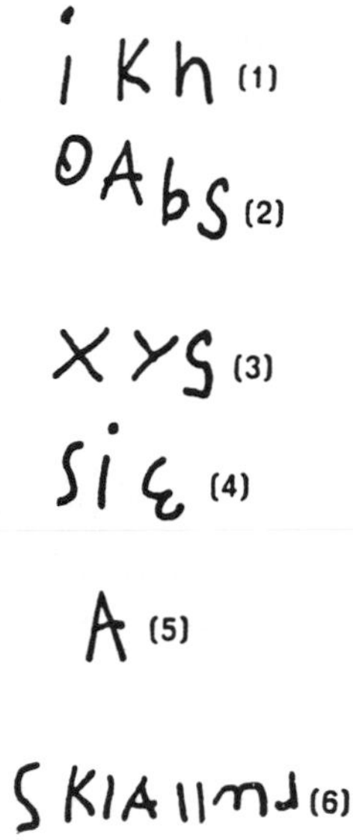

i Kh (1)

OAbS (2)

XYS (3)

Si ε (4)

A (5)

S KIA IImJ (6)

F R i O (1)

A i O A (2)

A O A (3)

A A O (4)

A O E (5)

A O (6)

B i B (7)

B O B (8)

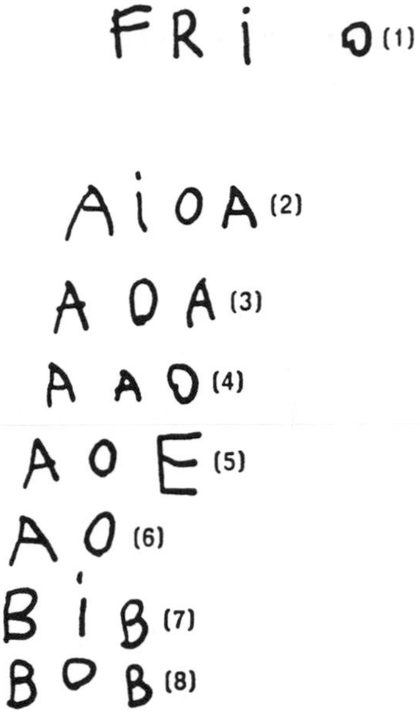

Figure 2.4
Example of Syllabic-Alphabetic Writing
(Julio Cesar, 6-years-old)

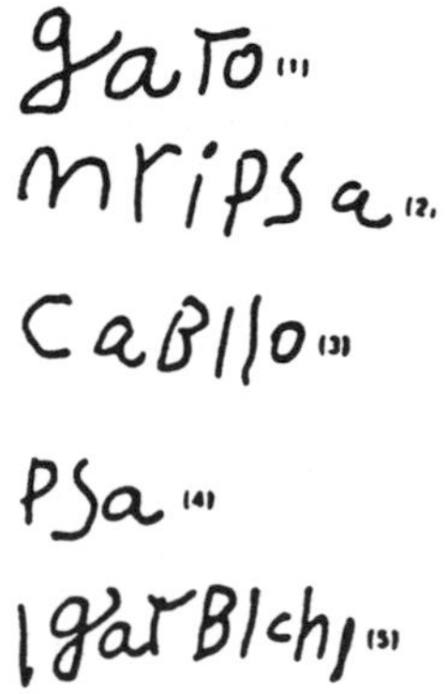

gaTo (1)

nrips a (2)

CaBllo (3)

PSa (4)

IgarBlchi (5)

44

CONCEPTUALIZATIONS OF WRITTEN LANGUAGE THAT UNDERLIE TEACHING PRACTICES

At the heart of the controversy in traditional approaches to the problems involved in the teaching of reading and writing lies the question of the method to be used: the analytic *versus* the synthetic method, phonics *versus* global approaches, and so on. The classical controversy does not take into account what we now know about the conceptualizations that children have regarding the writing system. For this reason, it is imperative that we examine teaching practices from a new perspective. If we are willing to accept that the child is not a tabula rasa upon which letters and words are going to be inscribed in the order determined by the method employed, that what is "easy" and what is "difficult" to learn must be defined from the perspective of the learner and not in terms of the adult, and that whatever information received must be assimilated (and therefore transformed) before the child may operate with it, then we must also accept that teaching methods (understood as a sequence of steps ordered in such a way as to attain a goal) can at best offer suggestions and hints (when they are not just reduced to the imposition of ritual practices or to a set of restrictions). The method cannot produce knowledge.

It is fundamental that we understand the problems as children pose them and the sequence of solutions they find acceptable (that give rise to new problems) before we can even imagine the kind of pedagogical intervention that should be designed to meet the real needs of the learning process. To reduce these interventions to what is traditionally designated as "the method employed" would put too great a restraint on our inquiry.

Instead of asking about the method employed, it is more useful to look at the *practices* used to introduce the child to written language, and how this object is presented in the

45

classroom.[10] There are practices that lead children to think that knowledge is something that *others* possess and that they must turn therefore to *others* to obtain it without ever participating in the construction of such knowledge. There are also practices that make them think that "what has to be known" is given once and for all, as if it were a closed, sacred, and immutable set of elements that are to be transmitted but not modified. Yet other practices place the children "outside" the knowledge, making them passive spectators or mechanical receivers who can never find the answers to the whys and wherefores that they don't even dare to formulate aloud.

There is no neutral pedagogical practice. Every single one is based on a given conception of the learning process and of the object of such a process. Most probably, those practices much more than the methods themselves are exerting the greatest lasting effects in the domain of literacy, as in any field of knowledge. Certain practices may appear "normal" and others "aberrant" depending upon how the relation between the subject and the object of knowledge is understood and how both terms of this relation are characterized. It is at this point that psychopedagogical considerations must be supported by epistemological reflections.

Our experience with in-service elementary teachers leads us to the identification of three main difficulties that need to be examined first if we want to change their views about literacy acquisition. First, the "naive" literate adult's view about the writing system. Second, the confusion between writing and drawing letters. Third, the reduction of the reader's knowledge to a knowledge of letters and their conventional sound values.

Let us take a brief look at the first two before examining the third in greater detail. There is no way in which we can hope to recover the vision we had of the writing system when we were illiterate (because we were all born illiterate!). Only through a knowledge of the psychogenetic process can we recreate the vision we all presumably had when we were children.

The confusion between writing and drawing letters (Ferreiro and Teberosky 1979/1982, Chapter 8) is, in turn, also quite difficult to shed light upon, because it is based on a view of the learning process that depends on the procedures of copying models repeatedly for its success. The best way of understanding the problems at the heart of this confusion is to study some of the many children who are perfect "copyists" but do not understand the rules of construction of the text they are copying.

It is common among literate adults to reduce the reader's knowledge to a knowledge of letters and of their conventional sound values. To put this view into question, we have, on many occasions, worked with a situation that produces an awareness almost immediately. We form small groups (of four or five people) and give them printed materials in unfamiliar writing systems (Arabic, Hebrew, Chinese, etc.), which we ask them "to read." Obviously, their first reaction is to reject such a task: How can they be expected to read them if they do not know those letters? We insist that they try. When they agree to explore the material, the exchange within the members of the groups begins almost immediately.

First, they discuss the classification of the object that they have in their hands: Is it a book (if so, what kind), a newspaper, a magazine, a pamphlet, or what? Once they have agreed on the classification, they begin to anticipate the organization of the content. If it is a newspaper, it must have sections (foreign and domestic affairs, sports, etc.); if it is a book, the title, the author's name, the printing press and the year of publication should appear at the beginning, and a table of contents at the back or the front. They invariably assume that the pages are numbered, which permits them to find the graphic distinctions between numbers and letters. In some cases, the orientation of the writing is not clear (from right to left or vice versa), and they proceed to search for some clues that will help them reach a decision (for example, to find where one paragraph ends and another begins). They also assume that there are upper- and lower-case letters and punctuation marks. They assume that a newspaper may be expected to appear with the complete date (day, month, and year). If the material contains photographs or drawings, they presume that the texts closest to them must contain information about them, and in the case of a well-known person (a politician, actor, sportsman, etc.), they assume that his/her name must be included in the text. If the same person appears in two photographs, they immediately search for something similar in what they presume are the captions, and if they succeed in finding it, they decide that this must be the name of the person in question. And so it goes on.

After about an hour of exploration, the groups reach their conclusions, which generally take the form of "This must mean . . ." and "We think that this means . . . because. . . ." Those who have made the most progress in the interpretation of their material are those who have found photographs, drawings or diagrams upon which they may base their interpretation. We tell them that young children do exactly the same thing. The members of the groups all feel very disoriented while exploring these unfamiliar characters, and they soon become aware of the problems involved in finding two identical characters when they do not know what is or is not relevant to distinguish between two or more graphic symbols. We then tell them that this is how children feel when they begin to learn. However, all these adult readers are able to hazard a guess at the meaning because they know what a book is, how it is organized, and what kinds of things are likely to be written in it (and the same goes for newspapers, magazines, and so on). As a rule, children do not have this kind of knowledge. Teachers also discover that making conjectures about the meaning and then attempting to find clues in the text to support this conjecture are complex intellectual activities, which are quite different from pure guesswork or wild imaginings. Thus, they discover that a reader's knowledge of written language cannot be reduced to knowledge of letters.

Once these initial conceptual difficulties have been

overcome, it is possible to analyze teaching practices in terms other than those of methodology. As an example, I shall analyze the conceptualizations about written language that underlie some of these teaching practices.

The Order in Which Reading and Writing Activities Should Be Introduced

This has always been a controversial issue. In Latin America, tradition advocates the introduction of both activities at the same time.[11] Despite this, it is expected that children will be able to read before they can produce their own written texts (without copying). Anyway, teachers continue to ask if it is safe to promote reading before writing. What is the correct order of these skills? If one believes that the objective of teaching written language is to learn a code of transcription, it is possible to divorce the teaching of reading from that of writing, since both entail different, though complementary, learning skills. However, there is absolutely no point in making this distinction when we realize that children's efforts are devoted to understand *the structure* of the writing system and, trying to do it, they carry out both activities of interpretation (reading) and production (writing). To divorce one activity from another is inherent in the view of the teaching of writing as the teaching of a transcription technique, and the skills associated with it.

The Way in Which Each Letter Should Be Presented

Whether the name or the sound of each letter should be stressed has also been a controversial issue. The same applies to the order in which letters and words should be introduced, which implies a sequence from the "easiest" to the "most difficult." I shall not attempt to discuss the definition of "easy" and "difficult" that I am using, though this is a fundamental problem[12] responsible for the initial failure in communication between teacher and student. Figure 2.5 illustrates this breakdown in communication very well.[13] (The difference between the animals should be understood as the difference in "systems" available to each, and the unequal distribution of power implicit in this difference.)

Figure 2.5
Breakdown in Communication
Between Teacher and Student

I shall discuss the assumptions underlying this only with respect to the information available. Written language is a cultural object that exists and is used in social situations (and not merely in educational settings). When children live in an urban area, they find written texts all over the place (public announcements on the streets, advertisements on food products, propaganda, writing on TV, etc.). Any urban environment is full of letters that do not appear in any predetermined order but in the order of frequency that corresponds to the writing of a given language. In addition, the letters of the environment are written in different styles and typographic characters. No one can prevent children from seeing them and paying attention to them. Similarly, no one can honestly expect children to rely only on their teacher for information; they are bound to ask other literate people who surround them (such as brothers, sisters, friends, relatives, etc.) for information.

When teachers decide the way in which letters are to be presented at school, they often attempt to control parental behavior in this respect at the same time (the typical invitations to cooperate in refraining from doing anything other than what the child is doing at school). Teachers may perhaps be able to control the parents, but it would be unrealistic to think that they could keep under control all the potential informants (brothers, sisters, relatives, etc.), and it is absolutely impossible to control the presence of written material in an urban environment.

The need to open the school to the community has been stressed often enough. Strangely enough, it is precisely when it is easiest to open it that we insist on closing it. Children observe more letters outside than inside school; they can try to interpret the texts they see outside as well as inside school; they try to write outside school because in school they are given permission only to copy and almost never to produce their own way to do it.[14] We need to acknowledge that environmental information has many points in common with the general linguistic information they received when they learned to speak. It is varied information, apparently disorganized, contradictory at times, but it is information concerning written language in its social context, while educational information is often presented out of context.

Underlying the controversy concerning the order and sequence in which letters should be presented is the conception of writing as a technique of transcribing sounds, as well as a more serious matter that may have many consequences: the transformation of writing into a pedagogical object, and, consequently, the conversion of the teacher into the only authorized informant.

We could continue to analyze, in a similar fashion, other educational practices, as clear indicators of the conceptions instructors have of the object and the process of learning. It is not an easy task to transform those practices, because both the teacher's role and the social dynamics within and without the classroom have to be redefined. It is worth pointing out that the above analysis does not allow us to conclude that the teacher

51

should merely become an observer of a spontaneous process.

Ana Teberosky, in Barcelona, was the first person to lead a pedagogic project based on what are, to my mind, three simple but fundamental ideas: (a) All environmental information available should form part of literacy classroom activities (a principle with heavy consequences, when it is taken seriously); (b) the teacher is no longer the only one who knows how to read and write in the classroom, given that each member of the class is recognized as able to read and write at his/her own level;[15] (c) the children who are not yet at the alphabetical level may help themselves and their peers when everyone in the classroom is able to discuss ways of dealing with written language, both in production and in interpretation activities. (See Teberosky 1982, for further details concerning this final point.)

FINAL REMARKS

It should be clear from the above discussion that the changes needed to deal with literacy acquisition from a new perspective *cannot* be reduced to a new teaching method, to the search of new reading-readiness tests or new didactic devices (particularly new primers).

What is needed is a change of perspective. We have had a very poor image of written language; to look at the alphabetical writing system as one of the ways to represent language helps us understand the complexities of the questions children formulate. We also have had a very poor image of the learner. Children are much more than a pair of eyes and ears, a hand that uses an instrument to make marks, and a phonatory machine that utters sounds. Beyond all this, there is a cognitive subject, someone who thinks, who constructs interpretative schemes, who acts upon reality in order to make it his/her own.

A new "magic" method will not solve the problem. What is needed is a new analysis of the actual school practices, trying to grasp their underlying assumptions and to determine up to what point they act as filters that selectively transform and distort any new proposal. Such an analysis would take us beyond the scope of this chapter.

Reading-readiness tests are not neutral either. Without going into the detailed analysis that would be required to uncover the assumptions on which these tests are based, I would like to point out that the "reading readiness" that these tests are supposed to assess is just as scarcely scientific a notion as the "intelligence" others attempt to measure.[16] There are turning points in history, at which a conceptual revolution is necessary. The time has come to make such a big conceptual change in literacy acquisition.

NOTES FOR EACH FIGURE

Figure 2.1a

A (Adult): What did you draw?
C (Child): A doll ("un muneco," a masculine noun).

A: Mark his name.
C: (She makes a zigzag line (1).)

A: What did you mark?
C: Ale (the diminutive form of her brother's name, Alejandro).

A: Please draw a little house.
C: (She draws a square with two lines inside, like a door.)

A: What did you draw?
C: A little house.

A: Mark its name.
C: (She makes a zigzag line (2).)

A: What did you mark?
C: Little house.

A: Do you know how to write your name?
C: (She draws four short zigzag lines (3).)

A: What did you mark?
C: Adriana.

A: Where does it say Adriana?

C: (Points vaguely to (3).)

A: Why does it have four pieces?
C: Because.

A: What does it say here (first segment of 3)?
C: Adriana.

A: And here (second segment of 3)?
C: Alberto (her father's name).

A: And here (third segment of 3)?
C: Ale.

A: And here (fourth segment of 3)?
C: Tia Picha (Aunt Picha).

Figure 2.1b

(1) pez (fish)
(2) el gato bebe leche (the cat drinks milk)
(3) gallina (hen)
(4) pollito (chick)
(5) pato (duck)
(6) patos (ducks)

Figure 2.2

(1) Carmelo Enrique Castillo Avellano (his own name, pointing to one letter for each noun)
(2) vaca (cow)
(3) mosca (fly)
(4) mariposa (butterfly)
(5) caballo (horse)
(6) mama come tacos (mummy eats tacos)

Figure 2.3a

In all the pieces of writing except the first and the fourth, each letter stands for one syllable.

(1) ga-to (cat)
(2) ma-ri-po-sa (butterfly)
(3) ca-ba-llo (horse)
(4) pez (fish)
(5) mar (sea)

(6) el-gat-be-be-le-che (the cat drinks milk)

Figure 2.3b

The vowels correspond, in general, to the correct vowel of each syllable.

(1) Fran(FR)-cis(I)-co(O)
(2) ma-ri-po-sa (butterfly)
(3) pa-lo-ma (pigeon)
(4) pa-ja-ro (bird)
(5) ga-to (cat, adding an extra letter, E, to have the preferred number of three letters)
(6) pa-to (duck, this time accepting the two letters)
(7) pez (fish) (dissatisfied with the result)
(8) pez (second attempt because he is not able to find a good solution. Only one letter is not a written word. . . .)

Figure 2.4

(1) gato
(2) mariposa
(3) caballo
(4) pez
(5) el gato bebe leche

Chapter 3

PRINCIPLES OF SPELLING FOUND IN THE FIRST TWO GRADES

by François Siegrist and Hermina Sinclair, University of Geneva

François Siegrist, Emilia Ferreiro, and Constance Kamii were Hermina Sinclair's students at the University of Geneva. Professor Sinclair, a collaborator of Jean Piaget, continues to be a mentor to her former students, and it is a special honor to include her in this book as one of the authors.

In this chapter, Siegrist and Sinclair describe a study that extended Ferreiro's work into the first two years of school. It showed that children beyond the alphabetic level (described by Ferreiro) do not all construct the writing system in exactly the same way but continue to manifest the constructive process.

Long after psychologists became interested in the acquisition of spoken language as an active, conceptual, and constructive process, written language continued to be treated only as an educational phenomenon. When psychologists considered the child's acquisition of written language, they thought merely of perceptual and motor skills necessary to become a producer and reader-aloud of script. When the mainstream of linguistics was historical, concerned with language change, written documents were of paramount importance. Twentieth-century general linguistics, by contrast, focused on spoken language as can be seen in statements such as "Writing is not language, but merely a way of recording language by visible marks" (Bloomfield 1933, p. 21), or more recently "It is one of the cardinal principles of modern linguistics that spoken language is more basic than written language" (Lyons 1981, p. 11).

Recently, however, matters have changed, and the study of written language has again become an object of study for linguists (Derrida 1967; Blanche-Benveniste and Chervel 1969; Catach 1978; Sampson 1985; Anis 1988; among others). This renewed interest in written language, from the point of view of its relation to the particular language it represents, brought to the fore several questions that are important when children's access to literacy is studied, even if the discussion is limited to the so-called alphabetically, or phonographically, written languages.

One such question is that of the distance between spoken and written language in general, which may vary across cultures and over time. As Sampson (1985) argues for English,

> The kind of English we use in writing and the kind we use in speech are, in the linguist's technical sense, closely-related dialects—that is, they both derive from a single ancestor language, which was spoken language. Literary English inherits all the apparatus of a spoken language, including phonology from its spoken ancestor, but it so happens that this particular dialect is not normally spoken (except when written documents are read aloud). (p. 27)

There are, indeed, many differences between written and spoken English, in word frequencies, use of pronouns, and verb forms, etc.

Another question concerns the degree to which written letters or digraphs correspond to sound segments that are actually produced in speaking. English and French are further removed from a strict correspondence than Spanish, Italian, or German. Many phonographically written languages introduce logographic/morphemic writing principles (that is, principles based on

58

meaning-bearing elements, rather than on sound) for various historical, etymological, and other reasons. For example, in English *missed* (phonetically identical to the noun *mist)* is written with the ending *-ed,* which has the morphemic value of the past tense of a verb.

Answers to these and related questions require careful analysis and comparison of different languages. Such studies are only beginning to appear, but these beginnings have already thrown a different light on the many problems children have to solve to become readers and writers.

Over the last twenty years or so, some psychologists have also begun to study the acquisition of written language as a complex system with which children are in contact from an early age. This perspective of examining the child's effort to find organizational principles in written language is very different from considering the process of learning only in formal schooling. Ferreiro (Ferreiro and Teberosky 1979/1982) was the first to study preschoolers' ideas about written language using Piagetian theoretical postulates and interviewing methods. She showed the internal coherence of the psychological process by which children gradually construct the basic phonographic principle of the alphabetic writing system. According to her findings, children assimilate information from the environment into their interpretative systems that change in a certain sequence, though cultural and socio-affective factors influence their onset and duration.

The longitudinal study reported here may be considered an extension of Ferreiro's work into the first two years of school, when children have grasped the basic phonographic principle but are still only beginning to learn orthography, that is, correct spelling. The study was carried out with French-speaking children, but despite many differences between the French and English writing systems, there are enough similarities for the results to be comparable. Certain problems children have to solve, and the way they go about solving them, may well be even

59

more general.

One of us (Siegrist 1986) had already shown that by the age of seven (first grade) most children in Genevan schools are able to produce written French that can be read aloud as meaningful texts by a reader who follows French rules for oralization. These texts are far from being correct orthographically, but the basic phonographic principle is clearly mastered in first grade. We also knew that subsequent progress in orthography could not be accounted for by a better command of phonographic correspondences. Indeed, Siegrist's research (in press) shows that, toward the middle of second grade, 91 percent of the children's written productions respect French phonographic correspondence, but that only about half the words are correctly spelled. Progress in third and fourth grades thus bears only exceptionally on this correspondence, and mostly on morphemic and etymological conventions, e.g., the -s ending of noun plurals (mostly silent in French) begins to appear regularly in third grade. The following study was carried out to get some idea of the constructive process at work during the first two years in school.

METHOD

Twenty children were seen six times when they were in first and second grade—once at the beginning of the school year, once in the middle, and once at the end. These sessions will be numbered 1 through 6 in the following discussion. Except for session 4, which was conducted with entire classes, the children were interviewed individually for about 30 minutes each time.

In the interviews, the children were asked to produce short texts. These were either dictated (somewhat longer sentences were used in second grade) or produced to correspond to a series of pictures. Other pictures (an elephant, three birds, four flowers, eight stars) were to be labeled. The dictated sentences incorporated words with silent letters (such as *honest*, de*b*t, and mak*e* in English), homophones (such as *right* and *write* in English), homonyms (a *ring* and to *ring* in English), necessary apostrophes (such as a *girl's* coat in English), and accented letters (é, à, and ç). The interviews were conducted according to the Piagetian exploratory method, with probing questions, requests for explanation, and sometimes counterarguments by the experimenter.

The youngest child was 6;1 (six years, one month), and the oldest 7;3 at the first interview in first grade. Ten of the 20 children were in one classroom; the other 10 were in another. The two groups thus had different teachers, and all the children in each class went from first to second grade as an intact group.

The teaching method in these classes left much freedom to the teachers, but was focused on the segmentation of spoken words and the various transcriptions that are possible in French. The children were encouraged to write and their early attempts were not sanctioned as "wrong" or "stupid," but corrections were gradually introduced and spontaneous attempts were valued for their content as well.

Each child's six protocols were analyzed as a record of his or her progress. The ten protocols of each group at each session were also inventoried as well as the 120 protocols of both groups over all the sessions.

RESULTS

Most productions followed French phonographic rules, although most of the words were incorrectly spelled. The many different ways phonemes can be transcribed by letters or letter-combinations in French (e.g., *o, ot, od, au, eau, eaud,* and *eaux* for /o/) make it possible to produce lengthy texts that do not transgress phonographic rules but in which all the words are wrongly spelled. A typical example is the following way of writing "six enfants boivent dans un verre (six children drink from a glass)" in session 4: "sis anfan boive dens un vairs." Despite this expected finding, an important difference was noted in the productions of the first three sessions. One approach was based on a focus on knowledge of spoken language, and the other was based on knowledge of written material. We elaborate on the two approaches below and conclude by showing that most subjects coordinated the two approaches in the last sessions. The following two ways of writing "The giraffe eats leaves" found in the data collected in the United States by M. and G. Manning *(Personal Communication,* April 1990) may help the reader anticipate our discussion:

"theJrifEtLES"
"the Jowraunf eat Lees"

Although some subjects in both classes more or less consistently took one approach, this was not true for all the subjects. Some children in both classes sometimes changed their centration from one session to the next or from one task to another. (A centration in the Piagetian sense refers to focusing on a specific aspect of an object-to-be-known that the subject tries to assimilate into his or her already existing structures.)

CENTRATION ON KNOWLEDGE OF SPOKEN LANGUAGE

This centration is characterized by the children using their knowledge of spoken French, and basing their writing on an auditivo-graphic correspondence, ignoring the special conventions of written texts, but producing a quite coherent and easily "readable" text. This centration is observable both in the spelling of single words and in the segmenting of texts. The following features can be singled out:

- Silent letters are almost always omitted: "pti" for "petit (small)."
- Diacritics (such as accents) are often omitted.
- Homophones (like *right* and *write)* are written identi-

cally: "ver" for both "vert (green)" and for "vers (toward)."

When asked questions about homophones, some children explain with great conviction that "one hears the same thing, so one writes the same."

As regards segmentation of sentences, the children seem to follow principles drawn from spoken language as well. They introduce no blanks between words at all in short sentences, and explain, when asked, "It's all one word." Below are two examples from sessions 1 and 2 respectively:

"Délapanmange"for "Des lapins mangent (Some rabbits are eating)"
"ilevelepie" for "il lève le pied (he lifts his foot)"

Interestingly, this centration leads the children to introduce one blank only in longer sentences, separating subject and predicate. This segmentation follows a metalinguistic intuition of the separation of a sentence into nominal phrase and verbal phrase that constitutes a much "deeper" segmentation than the blanks between words. In a sentence such as "The boy has eaten an apple," for example, the links between "the" and "boy," or between "an" and "apple," are much closer than those between "boy" and "has" or between "eaten" and "an," but the blanks are of equal size. Berthoud-Papandropoulou (1978) noticed similar intuitions in her metalinguistic studies. This syntactic intuition can be based only on children's metalinguistic reflection on spoken language, since no special segmentation of this kind is present in the written texts they see. Some examples are the following:

"lours nemepalabriko" for "l'ours (the bear) n'aimait pas l'abricot (did not like the apricot)"
"séonpetigason kitapeanchian" for "c'est un petit garçon (it's a little boy) qui tape un chien (who hits a dog)"

Another type of segmentation, also based on spoken language but not syntactic, is produced by children who separate each syllable (as also noted by Berthoud-Papandropoulou (1978) in her metalinguistic studies). An example is: "il la che une min a pré les deus" for "il lâche une main après les deux (he lets go of one hand after two, session 2)." Some segmentations seem to be the result of a focus on organizational principles derived from the observation of written material, such as blanks introduced between two identical letters. Indeed, children often judge that for written material to be "good for reading," identical letters should not be contiguous (see Ferreiro and Teberosky 1979/1982). This seems to be the reason for the blanks in the following examples: "gé étédomre" for "j'ai été dormir (I went to sleep, session 1)" and "tuva alécol" for "tu vas à l'école (you go to school, session 1)." The children who produced these examples made it clear during the interview that they were thinking of the way one has to speak precisely, introducing a hiatus between two vowels.

CENTRATION ON KNOWLEDGE OF WRITTEN LANGUAGE

This centration bears on what the child already knows about certain characteristics of written material that have no link with spoken language. As in the case of the first centration, this also results in observable features both of isolated written words and of sentences. Capitals are introduced here and there, *ph* appears in cases where a simple *f* is correct, "special" letters such as *c* are written, and trigrams such as *eau* for /o/ are introduced. This type of text appears less coherent than the phonographic transcriptions described above. Yet, there are already some words correctly spelled and correctly segmented, even those that often cause difficulties much later, such as words beginning with a vowel preceded by *l'*.

Below are examples of this centration:

"setes Fasil" for "c'était facile (it was easy, session 1)"

"Il Phé le fou" for "Il fait le fou (He is clowning, session 2)"

"qui jous aux deaumino" for "qui joue aux dominos (who plays dominos, session 3)"

In the first example, "setes" could be seen as an endeavor to write "c'était" phonographically. When the rest of this child's production is analyzed, however, and his remarks taken into account, it is more probable that "setes" represents a combination of two correctly spelled words—"se" and "tes" (a reflexive and a possessive pronoun).

The segmentation resulting from this centration appears much less coherent than that introduced by the phonographic centration. In general, blanks are introduced before and/or after a word the child already "knows," such as "il (he)," "un (a or an)," "les (the, plural)," "l'ours (the bear)," and "sous (under)." As one girl explained, "After little words you leave a space." This idea does not always lead to correct segmentation, however, and the following errors make the centration on the visual organization especially clear:

"le la Pin mamange" for "les lapins mangent (the rabbits are eating, session 1)."

This child split the noun *lapin* into *la* (feminine article) and *Pin* (pinetree, correctly spelled). *Mangent* has an extra syllable, making the well-known word *maman* (mommy) appear.

In general, this second approach results from attentive observation of salient characteristics of written texts and from the already acquired correct spellings for certain words. In contrast with the productions directed by the first centration, these texts are more difficult to read aloud and thus to understand. They have to be considered bit by bit rather than in their totality. This remark does not mean that such productions are less good than the others; they are different in the sense that their scriptors appear to be more sensitive to the logographic-morphemic aspect

65

of written French. As we shall see, from the fourth session onwards, the two centrations become coordinated.

COORDINATION

Two of our subjects showed relatively pure, contrasting centrations in first grade. In session 4 (first session in second grade), however, it became almost impossible to decide what their initial centrations were. Below is an example of an identical sentence written by the two children in session 4 when "ils vont vers le lavabo (they go toward the washbasin)" was dictated:

"ils vons ver le lavabot"

These productions are still incorrect enough to show the active construction the children apply to the task. It is also interesting to note that the two children were not in the same class and had different teachers. The convergence thus appears indeed to be due to an internal mechanism of coordination. Their total production in sessions 4, 5, and 6 shows that both phonographic correspondences and the particularities of French orthography are beginning to be integrated, though much still has to be acquired.

Silent letters appear but still not always correctly as can be seen in the unnecessary *t* at the end of *lavabo*. (One of the frequently found silent letters in French is *t*.) Segmentation is often correct, but difficulties remain, often with articles, as in the case of *l'eau* (water, with the *a* in the article *la* replaced by the apostrophe), and the negative particle *ne*. Silent letters, and the multiple possibilities of transcribing certain phonemes will remain difficult even for advanced writers. Knowledge of etymology helps, but not in all cases. There are many homophones that are written identically but many are not. Though there is a clear phonographic correspondence for many words, and though segmentation is determined by a coherent metalinguistic principle, other regularities can only be observed in correctly written texts (such as the frequent ending *emment* (adverbials), *tion* (Latin-derived nouns), *ent* (verb plurals), etc.).

It is this pluri-systemic character of written French, and of written English, that should lead us to consider both centrations discussed above as valuable approaches to the learning of orthography and to emphasize the necessity of their coordination. To return to "The giraffe eats leaves," the English sentence cited earlier, examples of coordination are "The garaf eats Leavs" and "the grAFE eats lefs." The almost total absence of haphazard spelling can be shown only by a careful analysis of each child's productions.

FINAL REMARKS

We hope to have shown that the various productions of our subjects over two years of schooling result from active constructions, guided by different centrations on the two facets of French orthography. Clearly, our subjects tried to organize their writing from an already acquired basic idea—that French is essentially written alphabetically, i.e., that there is somewhere a basic correspondence between phonemes and graphemes. Only a few subjects sometimes produced written forms that still departed from this principle. An example of such a departure is writing "c t" for "c'était (it was)." A similar example in English would be writing "i" for "eye" or "b" for "bee." (The letter *c* is called "say," phonetically identical to the syllable *cé,* and the letter *t* is called "tay," phonetically identical to *tait.*)

Such constructive activity has been demonstrated in many domains other than writing by Piaget and his collaborators. Kamii (1985, 1989) has shown it in another important school subject, arithmetic. It is, however, necessary to consider the many differences that exist between the fundamental concepts Piaget studied and conventional systems of representation. There are also fundamental differences among representational systems— between written language and written arithmetic, and among various systems of writing.

It seems nevertheless possible to consider the different centrations and their coordination as sketched above for French as being a characteristic of mechanisms at work in many other fields of knowledge, particularly orthography in other languages. Many of our subjects showed a consistency in their focusing on certain characteristics, and continued to apply them to an object of knowledge that at first appeared at least partially disorderly. Conflicts arise necessarily, but, as shown many times in Piaget's work, children, as knowing subjects, do not immediately abandon their theories or hypotheses when apparent contradictions arise. They may invent certain ad hoc solutions for conflicts, but these solutions lead to the construction of limited subsystems, which will eventually be assimilated one to the other and lead to a more adequate, integrated, and more encompassing system.

It is, of course, not possible to transpose the results of the study reported here into educational recipes. The pluri-systemic nature of written languages such as French and English is only beginning to be analyzed by linguists, and even if teachers were more aware of certain organizing principles that underlie both regularities and irregularities, this would not lead directly to methods of teaching that could make literacy in the full sense of the word easily accessible.

Nonetheless, the coherence of the productions of all our subjects shows both their capacity and their desire to come to grips with a difficult object-to-be-known. The mechanisms underlying children's search for coherence are similar to those shown by Piaget and his collaborators. The fundamental constructivist and interactionist view of Piagetian psychology appears to be a fruitful approach to a psychological study of writing. In this sense, the research reported here is indeed an extension of Ferreiro and her collaborators' approach to the study of preschoolers' construction of the writing system of their culture.

Chapter 4

SPELLING IN KINDERGARTEN: A CONSTRUCTIVIST ANALYSIS COMPARING SPANISH-SPEAKING AND ENGLISH-SPEAKING CHILDREN*

by Constance Kamii, Roberta Long, Maryann Manning, and Gary Manning, University of Alabama at Birmingham

The purposes of this study were to find out (1) whether English-speaking American children construct the same developmental levels in spelling as the Spanish- speaking children studied by Ferreiro and Teberosky (1979/1982) and by Ferreiro and Gómez Palacio (1982), and (2) whether English-speaking children, too, make their first letter-sound correspondences through syllables. The developmental levels were found to be very similar, but the English-speaking children were found to base their first phoneme- grapheme correspondences on consonants rather than on syllables. (See Note 8 of Chapter 2 for Ferreiro's call for further research on this point.)

*We would like to express appreciation to H. Sinclair (University of Geneva) for suggesting the questions raised for this study and for guiding us in data analysis. We would also like to acknowledge the assistance of B. Wolfson, who spent much time analyzing data and making helpful suggestions.

*The reader will note some differences be-
tween Ferreiro's three-level conceptualization in
Chapter 2 and the four levels described in the present
chapter. The reason for these discrepancies is that
Chapter 2 was written later, and this later
conceptualization was not available when the study
reported here was undertaken. The facts Ferreiro
found remain the same, but her later conceptualization, with intrafigural and interfigural considerations and the quantitative and qualitative axes,
serves as an example of how science, too, is
constructed by progressing from one level to the next,
according to Piaget (Piaget and Garcia 1983/1989).
This chapter appeared in the* Journal of Research in
Education, *vol. 4 (Spring/Summer 1990): 91–97.
Reprinted by permission of Constance Kamii,
Roberta Long, Maryann Manning, and Gary Manning, and the Association for Childhood Education
International, 11141 Georgia Avenue, Suite 200,
Wheaton, Md. Copyright © 1990 by the Association.*

Many researchers in America (Bissex 1980; Chomsky 1979; Henderson 1981; Read 1975) have shown repeatedly that young children "invent" spelling by going through several levels before constructing our conventional system. This research indicates that young children do not learn to spell by associating sounds and letters that are taught one after another. Accordingly, many kindergarten and first-grade teachers have changed from teaching formal phonics to supporting children's natural growth as writers.

While there is considerable knowledge about "invented" spelling, very little is known about children's earlier development from scribbling to "invented" spelling. The most systematic research available on this transition is that of Ferreiro and Teberosky (1979/1982), which was replicated with larger

70

samples by Ferreiro and Gómez Palacio (1982). Working in Argentina with Spanish-speaking 4- to 6-year-olds, Ferreiro and Teberosky based their research on the theory of Jean Piaget. According to Piaget, children begin to construct their knowledge about astronomy, meteorology, botany, and geology long before they go to school (Piaget 1926/1967). Ferreiro and Teberosky (1979/1982) hypothesized that preschool children must likewise have many ideas about how words are written. As part of this multifaceted research, Ferreiro and Teberosky asked four- to six-year-olds to write words that were familiar to them in written form (e.g., their own name and the name of a family member) and other words that were unfamiliar (e.g., sapo (toad), pato (duck), and oso (bear)). In subsequent analysis, the children's responses were conceptualized within five levels of development.

At level 1, children wrote strings such as those in Figure 4.1a. A characteristic of these strings is that they all look alike to the adult observer. To children at level 1, however, similarities among written words do not matter. What matters to them is their intent to write different words.

At the second level (Figure 4.2a), the children's writing revealed new ideas about how words are written. The children wrote words with a minimum and a maximum number of characters, or a fixed quantity of at least three characters. For example, the words in Figure 4.2a have a minimum of four and a maximum of five letters. The characters became more similar to conventional letters, and the children showed evidence of another important rule: Words have to look different if they are to be read. If their repertoire of letters was very limited, the children made the words look different by varying the order of the characters (see Figure 4.2a). We see here the construction of a system created by the child, as there is no rule in the external world stating that a word has to have a minimum and a maximum number of letters.

At the third level, the level of the syllabic hypothesis, the child used one character to represent each syllable, but the

Figure 4.1
Examples of Level 1

punishment

pop

cement

vacation

motion

vale/veil

umbrella

ocean

(a) Level 1 from Ferreiro and Teberosky's study

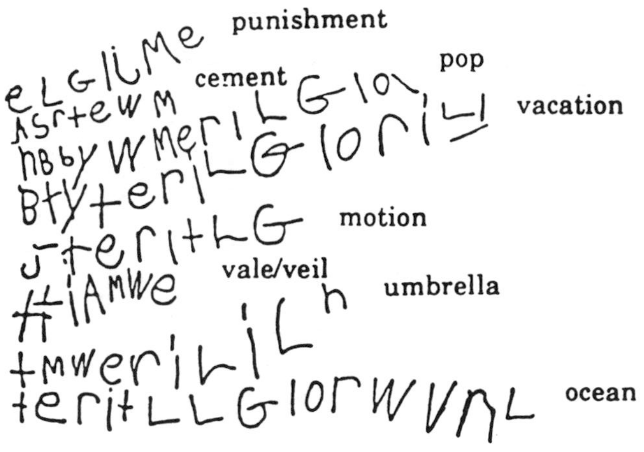

(b) Level 1 from our study

Figure 4.2
Examples of Level 2

(a) Level 2 from Ferreiro and
Teberosky's study

(b) Level 2a from our study

(c) Level 2b from our study

character did not have to have a phonetic value. Figure 4.3a gives examples of this syllabic writing for words such as sapo (toad) and patito (duckling). This level represents a major achievement because the child is showing for the first time the idea that written characters are related to sounds. Again, this is an internal construction of the child, as there is no rule in the environment stating that each character must stand for a syllable.

In another study, Ferreiro and Gómez Palacio (1982) found a second, more advanced type of writing within level 3 (Figure 4.3b). The child used each letter to represent not only a syllable but also the conventional vowel sound. Examples are "a o" for gato (cat) and "e a o" for pescado (fish).

Ferreiro and Gómez Palacio (1982) combined two levels (4 and 5) that had been delineated earlier by Ferreiro and Teberosky (1979/1982) and called it the syllabico-alphabetic level. We refer to the later publication, since it builds on the earlier research and is based on a much larger sample. As can be seen in Figure 4.4a, the child at level 4 sometimes continued to use each letter to represent a syllable but also began to make phoneme-grapheme correspondences. In "mriPSa" (mariposa, which means butterfly), for example, "m" and "P" are used to represent syllables, but "ri" and "Sa" are conventionally spelled. We can see here that syllabico-alphabetic writing develops out of the syllabic system.

Ferreiro and Teberosky's work (1979/1982) led us to wonder (a) whether or not English-speaking American children go through the same developmental levels as the Spanish-speaking children, and (b) whether English-speaking children, too, make their first letter-sound correspondences through syllables.

METHOD

The subjects of our study were 192 Alabama and Nebraskan kindergartners from five public schools. Their

Figure 4.3
Examples of Level 3

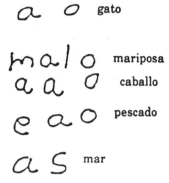

sapo

oso

patito

(a) Level 3 from Ferreiro and Teberosky's study

gato

mariposa

caballo

pescado

mar

(b) Level 3 from Ferreiro and Gómez Palacio's study
(the syllabic level with sound value)

punishment

cement

pop

vacation

motion

vale/veil

umbrella

ocean

(c) Level 3 from our study

75

Figure 4.4
Examples of Level 4

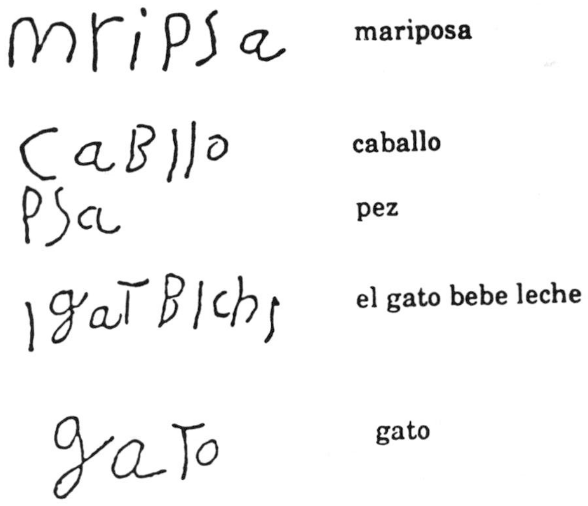

mripsa — mariposa

CaBllo — caballo
PSa — pez

1gaTBlchs — el gato bebe leche

gaTo — gato

(a) Level 4 from Ferreiro and Gómez Palacio's study

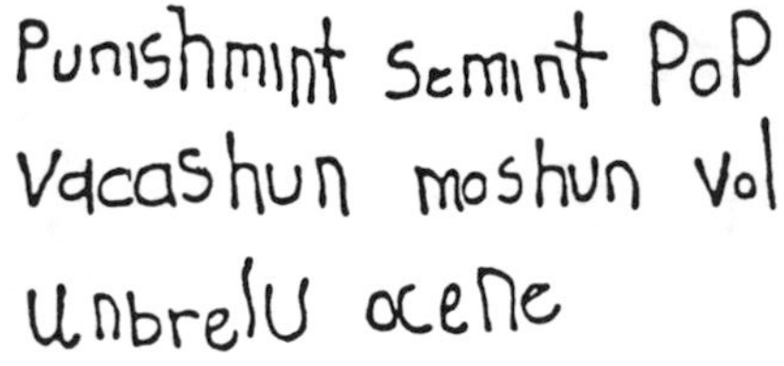

Punishmint Semint PoP
Vacashun moshun vol
Unbrelu acene

(b) Level 4 from our study

numbers according to SES were as follows: 30 suburban middle-class Caucasian children, 20 suburban middle-class Black children, and 47 urban lower-class Black children, all from Alabama. In addition there were 54 middle-class and 41 lower-class Caucasian children, from a small town in Nebraska. All of the children were receiving some instruction in reading and writing.

We asked each child to write the following eight words: "punishment," "cement," "pop," "vacation," "motion," "vale/ veil," "umbrella" and "ocean." This list consists of words that are familiar to most young children, and with the exception of "umbrella," do not appear in kindergarten instructional programs. It includes both monosyllabic and multisyllabic words; some words begin with consonants and others with vowels.

Each child was taken from the classroom and tested individually. After a brief conversation with the researcher, the child was given a blank sheet of paper and asked to write his or her name on it before being asked to write the eight words. Whenever necessary, questions were asked by the researcher to clarify the ideas underlying a production.

The children's writing was analyzed by four researchers, who categorized the writing according to Ferreiro and Teberosky's (1979/1982) criteria. If at least four of the eight words met the criteria for a particular level, the writing was categorized at that level. For example, in Figure 4.2c six of the words (punishment, pop, vacation, veil, umbrella and ocean) met the criteria for inclusion at our level 2b. Level 2b is explained in the section that follows.

RESULTS

The similarities and differences between the English-speaking and Spanish-speaking children are reported beginning with a level 0. In the Ferreiro and Teberosky study (1979, 1982), a few of the lower-class children refused to write; one child in our sample who refused to write also belonged to a lower-class group. Three of our children drew pictures when asked to write the words. For instance, when one child was asked to write ocean, she drew a circle with a boat in the middle. Since these children had not yet differentiated between drawing and writing (level 1), they were classified as level 0 (see Table 4.1).

Table 4.1
Kindergartners' Levels of Spelling

	Levels						
	0*	1	2a	2b	3	4	X
Number	3	13	40	21	89	14	11
Percentage	2	6	21	11	46	7	6

Total n = 192 (One child refused to write or draw.)
*Level 0 refers to children who drew pictures when asked to write words.

Children's writing was categorized as level 1 when they wrote strings of conventional letters without a maximum number of letters. While the strings of various lengths were similar to those in Ferreiro and Teberosky (1979/1982), the great majority of our children used conventional letter shapes, in contrast to children in the Ferreiro and Teberosky study. None of our subjects produced unconventional shapes and none of them produced similar or identical strings for different words.

We categorized children's writing as belonging to level 2 if four or more of the eight words written consisted of a fixed quantity or a minimum and maximum number of graphemes. For example, the words in Figure 4.2b have a fixed quantity of three letters, and those in Figure 4.2c have a minimum of three letters and maximum of five. At level 2 our findings were thus again similar to Ferreiro and Teberosky's (1979/1982). Our English-speaking pupils had constructed the same rule as the Spanish-speaking children and believed that a word must have a fixed number or a minimum and maximum number of characters, plus a variety of letters.

78

However, conventional letters already appeared in our level 1 as did the different appearance of the eight written words. Further, we found many words that met not only the criteria for level 2 but also another criterion: the "correct" first letter in each word. We found so many of these instances that we subdivided level 2 into levels 2a and 2b. Level 2a is illustrated in Figure 4.2b, and level 2b is illustrated in Figure 4.2c. Level 2b is characterized by instances when the correct first letter is used in at least half of the eight words written.

Although a few of our English-speaking children produced writing for one or two words that could have been considered syllabic, there was no evidence that any children had developed a general syllabic rule. We thus defined level 3 as consonantal because our children used only consonant letters for consonant sounds without writing any vowels. For example, many children wrote "pnmt" for "punishment," "cmt" for "cement" and "pp" for "pop" (see Figure 4.3c). By contrast, the Spanish-speaking children at level 3 wrote two squiggles for a two-syllable word and three squiggles for a three-syllable word (see Figure 4.3a). They sometimes wrote two vowels for a two-syllable word (e.g., "a o" for "gato" (cat) and three vowels for a three-syllable word (e.g., "a a o" for "caballo" (horse) as shown in Figure 4.3b).

At level 4, the Spanish-speaking and English-speaking children were again found to be similar. As can be seen in Figure 4.4b, level 4 in English also grows out of level 3. For example, in our study, children's writing of "pnmt" often became "punish-mint" and "cmt" often became "cemint." While the "mint" in "punishment" and "cement" is not yet conventional, it is consistent from one word to the next. The same is true of the "shun" in "vacashun" and "moshun." These consistencies suggest the presence of an alphabetic system approaching conventional spelling.

Finally, we observed a category X shown in Table 1 and illustrated in Figure 4.5b. In this category, the children wrote

Figure 4.5
Examples of One Letter for Each Word

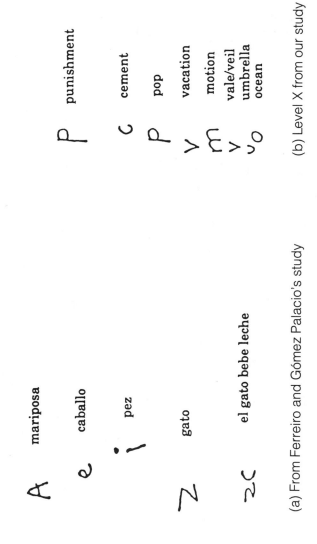

(a) From Ferreiro and Gómez Palacio's study

(b) Level X from our study

80

only the correct beginning letter for each word. Ferreiro and Gómez Palacio (1982) also reported a small category with only one letter or pseudo-letter for each word (see Figure 4.5a). However, in their study, there did not seem to be any indication that this letter corresponded to the first letter of the word.

DISCUSSION

Findings in our study are very similar to Ferreiro and Teberosky's (1979/1982), but there are three differences. First, children in our study made their first phoneme-grapheme correspondences by focusing on consonants, while the Spanish-speaking children focused on syllables. Second, children in our study wrote strings of conventional letters at level 1, instead of strings of letter-like squiggles such as those shown in Figure 4.1a. Third, in our study, children wrote so many correct initial letters at level 2 that we created an additional level called level 2b.

The major difference, that of the consonantal correspondence as opposed to the syllabic correspondence at level 3, can probably be explained by the nature of the differences between the two languages. Spanish differs from English in that syllables and vowel sounds are much clearer in Spanish than in English. English is primarily a stress-timed language in which vowel sounds and syllabic boundaries are clear only in stressed syllables. In unstressed syllables, the vowel phoneme is often reduced to the "schwa" sound. The result is many brief syllables which give the learner no sound cue for the appropriate vowel grapheme. Additionally, from the standpoint of phoneme-grapheme correspondence, Spanish is a much more consistent language than English. Moreover, many of the words frequently used by children such as "dog" (perro), "cat" (gato), "house" (casa) and "milk" (leche) are monosyllabic in English and multisyllabic in Spanish. In fact, very few monosyllabic content words exist in Spanish.

Our children wrote conventional letters instead of

squiggles at level 1 and produced many "correct" initial consonants at all levels. These differences are probably due to school instruction.

Level 2, both in English- and in Spanish-speaking children, is remarkable because no one teaches children that words have to be written with a fixed number of letters or with a minimum and a maximum number of letters. Level 3, the consonantal or syllabic level, is likewise remarkable because no one teaches such rules that children carefully follow. These rules suggest that children construct one coherent system after another as they try to make sense of the writing that they find in the environment. It is significant to note that almost all the children in our study wrote conventional letters but used them in a wide variety of ways at a variety of levels. The majority of the kindergartners we interviewed were at levels 2 and 3, but eight percent and seven percent, respectively, were found to use letters below and above levels 2 and 3. These findings attest to Piaget's theory that even social knowledge is not acquired directly by internalization from the environment. Social knowledge, too, is acquired by assimilation into the knowledge an individual already has and is constructed from within.

Detailed, longitudinal research is necessary to understand how children progress from one level to the next. In addition, we need to know how schools can intervene in kindergarten and the primary grades to produce the best results. Children need information, but they can assimilate it only at their own levels. It is, therefore, important for us to refrain from high-pressure instruction that may result in confusion or loss of confidence. If we foster children's curiosity and desire to read and write, they are likely to do better than if we impose isolated bits of information on them.

Chapter 5

LEARNING TO READ IN NEW ZEALAND

by Brian Cutting, Auckland, New Zealand, and Jerry L. Milligan, Washington State University

According to a recent study, New Zealand is the most literate country in the world. By contrast, the United States is 49th among the 159 countries of the world.

The authors compared how literacy is taught in the two countries. They point out that New Zealand educators see no need for systematic skills instruction and do not use basal readers and the accompanying workbooks and worksheets. Beginning reading instruction in New Zealand is a balance of five approaches: shared reading, reading to children, language experience, independent reading, and guided reading.

Literacy instruction in New Zealand is dominated by the whole-language philosophy, but they do not use the term "whole language." Many of the practices that American whole-language teachers use, such as the shared book experience, were developed in New Zealand.

The success of New Zealand's literacy instruction provides strong evidence in support of

Reprinted with permission of the publisher, Early Years, Inc., Norwalk, Connecticut 06854. From the August/September issue of *Teaching K–8*.

whole language. This kind of evidence is much more convincing than the interminable debates about the "Great Debate."

There is at the present time an increasing concern in the United States about the rate of reading failure and the general level of literacy as compared to other industrialized nations. In light of this concern, it occurred to us that it might be useful to identify a country where reading is taught more effectively, go there and observe firsthand how it's done.

New Zealand was chosen for an obvious reason: It is considered to be the most literate country in the world. The United States, according to a recent study, ranks 49th in literacy among the 159 countries of the world.

It should be noted that comparing the ways beginning reading is taught in the two countries is complicated by the fact that beginning reading is taught in diverse ways in the United States. For example, we found many classrooms in the United States where the approach was closer to the approach used in New Zealand than to the one used in most American classrooms.

In contrast, New Zealand has a single national school authority whose policies on reading instruction apply throughout the country. Thus, the small variations found in New Zealand classrooms must be attributed to differences in teachers, not policies.

With that in mind, let's take a look at some of the most significant differences.

AGE OF BEGINNING READERS

In the United States, formal reading instruction usually begins early in the first grade. Since most states require a child to be five or older before entering kindergarten, most first graders are at least six by the time they receive formal reading instruction.

New Zealand children, however, are permitted to enter

school on their fifth birthday. And, as we will discuss later, they receive reading instruction on their first day of school. The only children beginning school on the first day of the school year are those who had summer birthdays.

We found that New Zealand educators value the system of having the school year begin with a small group of five-year-olds which gradually increases in size until the group is somewhat over 30. They believe that this arrangement allows them to provide for more individualized instruction. Indeed, it forces individualized instruction.

READING READINESS

Most children in the United States receive prereading instruction prior to formal reading instruction. This instruction normally takes place during kindergarten and the beginning of first grade, and usually focuses on what American educators refer to as reading readiness—for example, developing such skills as visual discrimination and letter recognition.

In New Zealand, there simply isn't time for reading readiness. Reading instruction begins the very first day that children enter school. An effort is made to have the children impress their families by taking home a book they can read very soon after they enter school. The book is likely to be a short one that they have heard read aloud regularly and have read in unison with a fluent reader until they nearly know it by heart.

BEGINNING READING

The prevailing approach to beginning reading in the United States is the word-centered skills approach. The focus here is on enabling young readers to recognize an increasing number of words and on providing children with the skills they need to unlock words they do not recognize by sight so they can derive meaning from print.

Reading instruction in New Zealand is predicated on a

holistic theory of language teaching methods. What is known as the whole language approach is the policy throughout New Zealand. Any deviation from this approach is regarded as being counter to policy.

In practice, the word-centered skills approach used in the United States involves breaking language into small units such as words and parts of words, and then teaching these units in a planned sequence of skills developed. In contrast, reading instruction in New Zealand is based on the assumptions that children can best learn to read by reading, and that reading improvement comes mainly as a result of reading.

BALANCED READING

New Zealanders refer to their beginning reading program as a balanced reading program. This program is comprised of five approaches which are part of the teaching routine nearly every day. Each of these approaches serves a specific purpose.

Reading to Children is used, in both New Zealand and the United States, to demonstrate to children that reading can be a source of delight and to familiarize them with book language and story structure.

Shared Reading, with its goal of having children read aloud without the support of either teacher or classmates, is clearly aimed at building the young reader's enthusiasm and self-confidence.

The *Language Experience Approach* introduces five-year-olds to writing and crystalizes their concepts of words, sentences, letters and other conventions of language.

Guided Reading leads children to know reading as a process of actively reconstructing meaning by predicting one's way through print, not as a process of recognizing words.

Independent Reading is, of course, an end in itself. One feature of this approach is that reading is made as pleasant as possible. In a New Zealand classroom, one will see stuffed chairs and sofas, carpeted areas and many large pillows. Also, children are free to seek assistance from either the teacher or a classmate when they need help in making sense out of what they're reading.

READING MATERIALS

Big books are an integral part of beginning reading instruction—particularly the shared reading approach—throughout New Zealand. Upon entering school, a child becomes part of a small group of pupils gathered together by the teacher. The teacher reads aloud from a big book and while reading, points to the print and pictures.

We observed both teacher-made as well as commercially-prepared big books being used. The print in these books is large enough to be seen easily by a fairly large group of children. The pictures, particularly in the commercially-prepared big books, are colorful, while the language is predictable and often humorous and rhythmical.

Most of the commercially-prepared big books are also available in regular size paperback texts, which the children can take home to impress friends and family with their reading.

In addition to the big books, teachers in New Zealand use a variety of regular size books containing a single story, multiple copies of books containing poems or chants, and books (mainly paperbacks) containing poems and short stories. The journals written by the children as part of the Language Experience Approach are also a source of reading material.

READING RECOVERY

Although the term *remedial reading* is not a term New Zealand educators would likely use, they do have a program for six-year-olds that one might consider remedial. They refer to this early intervention program as *reading recovery*.

The reading recovery program is based on the assumption that it's better to prevent reading difficulties than treat them.

87

As many as 30 to 50 percent of the children in some schools receive, as they reach their sixth birthday, what is known as the *six-year-check*, a formal observation of children's orientation to print. As a result of the six-year-check, about 15 percent of the children, depending upon the school, may receive help from special teachers outside the classroom for part of their second year in school.

It should be kept in mind that this special help is provided during the children's seventh year of life. In the United States, it is not until the children' seventh year of life that formal reading instruction is begun.

FINAL THOUGHTS

From studying the development of reading instruction in the two countries, it is apparent that the differences have become institutionalized. Administrators and teachers in New Zealand grew up in a school environment dominated by the whole language philosophy. Since they learned what they needed to know about reading *from* reading, they do not see the need for systematic skills instruction.

While basal readers and other controlled vocabulary have been an integral part of reading instruction in the United States since early in this century, they have not been in New Zealand. Nor have the workbooks and work sheets which accompany basal series. The teachers fail to see the merits of basals and workbooks because this is not the way they learned.

At the present time, American educators are divided in their views regarding beginning reading instruction. While they debate such issues as phonics instruction and the best way to introduce decoding skills, New Zealand educators do not seem to be divided. They all seem to agree that beginning reading instruction should be a balance of the five approaches described earlier.

Finally, teachers colleges in New Zealand appear to be

much more involved with schools than in the United States, and they all seem to be advocating the same type of beginning reading instruction. This makes the preparation of teachers easier and tends to produce teachers who have similar views about the way reading should be taught.

Chapter 6

SHARED BOOK EXPERIENCE: TEACHING READING USING FAVORITE BOOKS

by Don Holdaway, International Education Consultant

This chapter is about shared book experience according to its title, but it sketches a much larger picture of the adoption of whole language, including shared book experience, as a national policy. (However, the term "whole language" is not used in New Zealand.) Of particular significance is the fact that this change came about in part because the old method was not working with children of minority groups—Polynesian immigrants from the Pacific Islands and Maoris.

Holdaway, the "father" of shared book experience, is explicit in his rejection of classical reinforcement theory. Speaking of the traditional method, he states, "We attempt to motivate children artificially and reward them extrinsically, neglecting the deep satisfactions which spring naturally from a proper engagement with books of high quality."

Teachers in the United States are also finding that shared book experience using "big books" is effective in beginning reading programs. Those who are using "big books" with low-income minority students are also enthusiastic about the value of shared book experience.

This chapter appeared in Theory Into Practice, *vol. 21, no. 4 (Autumn 1982):293–300. Reprinted with permission.*

Most children would agree that listening to stories is a most enjoyable activity, especially during the early years of schooling. Most teachers do read to their children and they, too, enjoy the experience. By contrast, the *instructional* reading program, however, does not seem to be characterized by anything like the same level of enjoyment for either children or teacher—it is often a time of boredom or stress and the ritualistic performance of unmotivating activities. Story time and reading time have different purposes, different content, and different rewards. They are so different that one must ask, "which best embodies literacy?"

As teachers, we tend to take the differences between these two situations for granted: story time is for pleasure and nothing—least of all word-solving—should be allowed to break the spell; reading time is for learning to read and is a necessarily difficult and painful activity for many children, requiring hard work and application—no spellbinding here. For the work of learning to read we attempt to motivate the children artificially and reward them extrinsically, neglecting the deep satisfactions which spring naturally from a proper engagement with books of high quality. We accept the structured materials provided for instruction without questioning their lack of intrinsic interest or worth.

Most surprisingly for an intellectually oriented institution like the school, we assume that problem solving—represented in reading by such "skills" as word-attack and in written language by such skills as spelling and calligraphy—cannot possibly be a rich source of pleasure. In contrast, we know by simple observation that the stumbling approximations of infants as they attempt to solve the problems of walking or talking *do*, in fact, provide them with immense pleasure, but we are so myopic in our observation of reading behavior that we fail to register the intense joy which may be experienced by children in solving the most basic problems of literacy. Before long the reading program has so completely excluded such forms of joy that they are no longer there to observe. To turn a topical Australian phrase, literacy, inasmuch as it has anything to do with life, wasn't meant to be easy.

Children who are already reading and writing when they enter school at 5, or who are so ready to learn that they take literacy in their stride, have had a rather different introduction to the real processes of literacy. Some of their deepest satisfactions for several years have centered around their fumbling but excited attempts to read, write, and spell. Almost invariably they are familiar with a wide range of favorite books which, to use one of Bill Martin's delightful phrases, they can "zoom through with joyous familiarity" (1972).

These are the books they loved so much that they pestered people to read to them again and again. These are the books which they played at reading to themselves, puzzled and pored over with aggressive curiosity about the devices of print. In this naturally joyful activity they learned rapidly about the mysterious relationships between fascinating language and pages of print. Their learning from these loved books was self-selected, intrinsically rewarded, and highly individualized.

Although story time in primary classes tends to be as enjoyable as it is in the book-loving home, it is not so effective in producing this "favorite book syndrome," and this is so for a number of reasons. There is not the same opportunity for personal selection. The teacher is not so free to respond to clamoring requests to "read-it-again." There is seldom the opportunity for all the children to handle the books independently as they become favorites. Because of visual and tactile distance from the text, there is not the same tendency for children to become curious about print at the crucial moments when they are reveling in the sounds of the language, nor is there the opportunity for them to point with their little fingers to details in the text and ask pointed questions. However, despite these losses in providing some of the crucial conditions to turn enjoyed books into favorite books, story time is still a powerhouse of natural motivation. Sadly, its output is largely wasted as a reinforcement for healthy reading behavior.

THE ADVENT OF SHARED BOOK EXPERIENCE PROCEDURES

About 15 years ago a group of teachers and academics in Auckland, New Zealand, began to take this natural literacy-learning situation very seriously. They were stimulated by a new challenge presented by a rapidly growing migrant movement of Polynesian people from the Pacific Islands and Maori people from rural districts into inner city schools. They were supported by a particularly lively climate of research and educational enthusiasm which was articulated throughout the system from department officers to practicing teachers, from university personnel to student teachers. They began cooperating and experimenting in new ways while maintaining healthy patterns of both criticism and support. The teaching procedures which began to develop and to be clarified in the ensuing years came to be known as "shared book experience." These procedures were integrated with already well-developed techniques in language experience approaches forming a complementary body of insights and techniques rather than a new methodology.

We were concerned to transform the educational context of the school in such a way as to achieve two goals.

a. To make available the most efficient learning environment possible in which to achieve literacy readiness for five-year-olds who did not come from literacy oriented backgrounds, and without segregating them from those who did.
b. To make entry into literacy a more natural and

94

successful process in which children of widely differing backgrounds could make optimum progress without developing a sense of failure in the first years of schooling.

The prevailing model for literacy-learning was failing to provide a satisfactory structure for a large proportion of children, especially those from cultural backgrounds widely different from the culture of the school. We wished to avoid those aspects of traditional approaches which highlighted invidious comparisons among children, such as lockstep movement through a series of readers. We were looking for procedures to develop competence in written English, without forcing children to regard their own spoken dialects as wrong or inferior. We were, as well, looking for procedures which teachers could readily use and understand.

Our studies indicated that under suitable motivation and in a favorable learning environment children would master literacy skills in a way very similar to that in which they master other developmental tasks, especially those of spoken language. The adults involved in providing the conditions for such natural learning do so without expert, academic knowledge, with justifiable optimism and with evident personal reward. It might, after all, be possible to approach these ambitious goals we set for ourselves.

A DEVELOPMENTAL EXPEDITION

The magnificently successful processes of learning spoken language in infancy provided the central model for the project and in an important sense provided justification for many thinly researched conclusions. What follows should be understood as implying that the spoken language learning model has been taken very seriously, and we know of no evidence that it is improperly applied to literacy learning.

One of the features of early research and development in this project was a determined attempt to study and understand the learning background which produces children who become high-progress readers in their first year at school. As with the spoken language model, this study leads us into a fascinating field of natural, developmental, pre-school learning. It is remarkable how little was really known 10 years ago about the conditions which produced our literacy-oriented children. Everyone agreed that it was a "good thing" to read to young children, and joked tolerantly about their tiresome demands to hear their favorite stories read again and again, but that's about it as far as it went. Everyone talked about pre-reading skills and programs without reference to the learning situations which actually produced the most literacy-ready children at school entry. A more systematic study of pre-school literacy activities soon highlighted some surprising features.

First, book-handling activities began at a very early stage, expanding the child's exposure to special forms of language and special types of language process long before the tasks of spoken language were mastered. These children began experimenting with book language in its primary, oral form while they were still using baby grammar and struggling with the phonology of speech. Yet it seemed an ideal time for this exposure and experiment. The sooner book-oriented activities began, the more likely it was that book-handling and experimental writing would become an important part of the daily preoccupations of the infant. Literacy orientation does not wait upon accomplished spoken language.

Second, the literature made available by ordinary, sensible parents to their children, even before the age of two years, was remarkably rich in comparison to "readers" used in the first year of school. They often included highly structured or patterned language of a repetitive, cumulative, or cyclic kind. Although the adults always seemed willing to attempt to explain new vocabulary, meanings, and idioms, the stories usually carried growing understanding from their central human concerns, and the adults were seldom worried about making certain their children understood every last word, or that they had direct sensory experience of every new concept. Just as speech develops in an environment which is immensely more rich than the immediate needs of the learner, so the orientation to book language develops in an environment of rich exposure beyond the immediate needs of the learner. In both situations, the learner selects appropriate items from the range.

Third, by determining *which* books they will have repeated experience of, children are involved in selection of those book experiences which will deeply preoccupy them from the earliest stages. The request to "read it again" arises as a natural developmental demand of high significance and an integral part of book exposure. Furthermore, in the behavior described in ensuing paragraphs, children quickly avail themselves of the opportunity to practice and experiment with a selection from the material made available to them. As in the mastery of other developmental tasks, self-selection rather than adult direction characterizes the specific and intensive preoccupations of early literacy orientation.

ROLE PLAYING AS READER—A NEGLECTED FEATURE OF LITERACY LEARNING

By far the most interesting and surprising aspect of preschool book experience is the independent activity of these very young children with their favorite books. Almost as soon as the child begins to be familiarized with particular books by repetitive experience, self-motivated, reading-like behavior begins. Attracted by the familiar object, the child picks it up, opens it, and begins attempting to retrieve for himself some of the language and its intonations. Quite early this reading-like play becomes story-complete, page-matched, and picture-stimulated. The story tends to be reexperienced as complete semantic units transcending sentence limits.

The time spent each day in these spontaneous attempts to retrieve the pleasurable experiences of favorite books is often greatly in excess of the time spent in listening to books being read by the adult(s) being emulated. The child attends for surprisingly long periods of time until the experience has achieved a semantic completeness, and the process may be repeated immediately with the same or another book.

A superficial assumption about this reading-like behavior would be that it was a form of rote learning based on repetitive patterning without deep comprehension or emotional response; that it would produce attempts at mere surface verbal recall. However, detailed study of this behavior through the analysis of tape recordings did not bear this out. On the contrary, what was displayed was a deep understanding of and response to central story meanings. The younger the child, and the less verbally competent, the greater was likely to be the distance from the surface verbal features of the text. The responses often involved what could only be called translation into forms of the language more typical of the child's current stage of linguistic development.

Here are two brief examples of this behavior at different levels of development.

Damion, age 2.0 years, retrieving *Are You My Mother?* by P. D. Eastman.

	Text	Responses
4	The egg jumped. "Oh, oh!" said the mother bird. "My baby will be here! He will want to eat."	Ow ow! A mummy bird baby here. Someping a eat ("a" used throughout to replace "to" and "for").
6	"I must get something for my baby to eat!" she said. "I will be back." So away she went.	Must baby bird a (i.e., "to") eated Dat way went. Fly a gye.

8 The egg jumped. It jumped and jumped! Out came the baby bird.	Ig jumped and jumped! Out baby bird!
10 "Where is my mother?" he said. He looked for her.	Whis my mudder? She look a her and look her.
12 He looked up. He did not see her. He looked down. He did not see her.	Her look up, look down. See her. (Damion cannot yet form a negative so he uses the affirmative in all such cases, adding a special intonation and a *shake of the head!*)

Far from producing the text in parrot-like fashion, Damion is guided by deep meanings to perform brilliant translations of meaning into baby grammar, displaying what have come to be known as "pivot structures."

Lisa-Jane, 4.0 years, from the same book:

34 The kitten and the hen were not his mother. The dog and the cow were not his mother. Did he have a mother?	So the pussy wasn't his mother. The hen wasn't his mother. The dog wasn't his mother. The cow wasn't his mother. And the baby bird said, "Did I have a mother?" and he DID!
36 "I did have a mother," said the baby bird. "I know I did. I have to find her. I will. I WILL!"	What a sad face. That one says: Did he have a mother? Did he have a mother? HE DID!

Note how on page 34 reported speech is transposed into direct speech and the converse is carried out on page 36. Note also that the side comment, "That one says," is an indication that Lisa-Jane knows the story comes from the print. She also has perfect control of the registers of both conversation and book language, and can change readily from one to the other.

The remarkable thing about the developmental difference between the 2- and the 4-year-old is not that it is different in kind, but that it is different in the degree of syntactic sophistication—an expression of the level of syntactic control available in deep processing. Both children start from whole-story understanding and retrieve in sentence units encoded into an appropriate syntax at the level of their spoken language development. Neither has memorized the vocabulary or the grammar word for word—they have memorized the meaning.

Approximation is a ruling principle, just as it is in learning spoken language. It should not come as a surprise—but to many it does—that these two learning situations in developmental behavior display classical reinforcement theory more clearly than any but highly contrived situations in school. Here is perfect exemplification of immediate reinforcement for every approximation in the right direction which learning theory recommends to us so strongly. Far from it being the case that developmental or "play" learning is something inferior to organized learning which sets up rigorous and efficient contingencies, developmental learning, in its almost flawless control of learning contingencies, puts the classroom to shame. We should not be saying that developmental learning is a hit-and-miss affair, lacking the efficient guidance and control provided in the school environment. It is *so* efficient and delicately controlled that we should, as teachers, be approximating towards that right learning structure. Yet we allow almost no place for approximation in learning to read, write, or spell.

Another noteworthy feature of this reading-like behavior is that it lacks an audience and is therefore self-regulated, self-corrected, and self-sustained. The child engages in this behavior without being directed to do so, at just those times when the loved adult is *not* available to do the reading. The child is not self-conscious or over-awed by the need to please an adult, nor is the child dependent on the adult for help or correction. Clay (1972) has shown how important the self-corrective strategy is to success in the early stages of reading.

To summarize, the bedtime story situation should not be separated from the independent output behavior which it generates. Such behavior normally engages the infant in extensive self-monitored, linguistic behavior for longer periods of time than are spent in the input activity of listening. The input and the output activities are complementary aspects of the same language-learning cycle. In both aspects there is close visual and tactile contact with the book, becoming increasingly oriented to print detail. All of the most powerful strategies of mature reading are being established and practiced in the reading-like, output behavior. The complexity and sophistication of the processes being mastered make the normal corpus of pre-reading skills look quite ridiculous.

There is obviously a great deal of positive reinforcement provided by both the input and output activities. In the first is the pleasure and delight of listening to the familiar human voice, full of warm intonation and bringing meaning to the special language where it differs from conversational language. The situation is socially rewarding, giving pleasure to both the adult and the child. It is a secure situation associated with proximity to our bodily contact with the adult.

The output activity is equally rewarding. Success in recreating the story is rewarded in a continuous, cyclic fashion similar to the rewards of experimenting with speech, and therefore tends to be self-sustaining. It is a situation which recalls the secure, pleasurable presence of the loved adult, and provides recall of the explanatory comments and answers to questions in the input sessions. The experience builds confidence in the ability to control language without outside help and, by the absence of criticism or correction, encourages self-regulation of complex language tasks.

In this situation, we have a further model for literacy-learning consistent in every way with the model derived from learning spoken language. Furthermore, it is the actual model demonstrated in the learning of those children who become our high progress readers or who teach themselves to read before entering school. In the model, the adult does not give instructions which the learner then attempts to carry out: rather, the adult provides real experience of the skill in joyful use. The skill then becomes a central feature of the learner's natural play and natural striving.

The early stages in the development of any complex human skill is activity which is *like* that skill and approximates progressively toward an activity which incorporates real processes and operations in mature use of the skill. Appropriate processes and strategies provide the foundation for successful practice and refinement—practice and refinement do *not* lead to the mature processes and strategies.

For literacy these strategies include:

- A deep, meaning-centered drive.
- Predictive alertness which harnesses background abilities such as syntactic responsiveness, semantic purposefulness, and experiential meaningfulness.
- Confirmatory and corrective self-monitoring by which output is constantly compared with sound models in prior experiences.
- Self-regulating and self-corrective operations leading to reinforcement patterns which are largely intrinsic and maintain high levels of task attention without extrinsic intervention.
- Risk-taking by approximation and trial backed by these sound strategies of self-monitoring.

(More detailed examples and implications are given in Holdaway 1979.)

APPLICATION TO CLASSROOM TEACHING

This model of natural, developmental learning in language could provide a powerful framework for a literacy program if the application to classroom conditions could be worked through. Such a program would be meaning-centered and process-centered rather than word-centered. It would be based on books from a wide literature which had become favorites for the children through enjoyable aural-oral experience. It would promote readiness in powerful ways associated with books and print, and would allow for a gradual transition from reading-like behavior to reading behavior. Approximation would be rewarded, thus supporting the early development of predictive and self-corrective strategies governed by meaning, which are crucial to healthy language use.

All of these factors seemed to be pointing in quite different directions from current methods, although they shared many features with language-experience approaches. We decided to take the model seriously and, at least for the purposes of exploration, see if it were possible to build a literacy program in which these principles were given genuine priority.

A growing body of psycholinguistic and developmental research seemed to be pointing in similar directions but a classroom methodology had not been worked out (e.g., Goodman 1968). Early work in individualized reading, led by Jeannette Veatch (1959), had broken much of the ground and provided valuable practical pointers, but teachers had been wary of this movement. In our own country, the work of Sylvia Ashton-Warner (1963) among rural Maori children had provided a useful debate and a persuasively documented account of classroom procedures consistent with many of the principles we were seeking to embody. In the United States, Bill Martin had begun to publish the materials which led to the Holt Rinehart *Sounds of Language* series, and we were certainly on the same wavelength. We gained much from a study of all of these movements.

What was missing from this rich body of knowledge about developmental teaching was some set of procedures whereby all the important aspects of the bedtime story cycle

103

could be replicated in the classroom. How was it possible to provide the same impact, the same level of participation, the same security and joy, the same prominence of print when there were 30 children rather than one? As so often happens, however, once the priorities had been set up, practical applications fell into place quite simply.

Three requirements needed to be met in order to achieve comparable or stronger impact than is achieved in the ideal pre-school, home setting. First, the books to be used in the reading program needed to be those that had proved themselves as loved by children. In this respect we, as teachers, had many advantages over parents both in determining which books children enjoy most and in obtaining them. We soon had some 200 titles, largely from the open literature rather than from reading schemes, known to be loved by 5- to 7-year-olds.

Second, the books needed to have comparable visual impact from 20 feet as a normal book would have on the knee of a child. This requirement was met by using enlarged texts. We made "blown-up" books about 30 inches by 24 inches—mainly from brown paper. Every child in a class group could see the print very clearly without needing to strain and press forward. Other devices such as charts, overhead transparencies, and projected slides were also used. Here again we found advantages over the home situation in that pointing and identifying details in an enlarged text suited the undeveloped muscular coordination of beginners.

Third, the teacher needed to present new material with wholehearted enjoyment, rather more as a performance than would be the case with most parents. The professional training of teachers normally ensures that this is a task they can carry out with skill and conviction.

Achieving the same level of participation as may occur in the one-to-one setting proved more difficult because only one question or comment could be fielded at a time. However, there were social compensations which far outweighed this limitation.

Provided the children could engage in unison responses where it was natural and appropriate, we found that all the ancient satisfactions of chant and song were made available to sustain the feeling of involvement. Indeed, by using favorite poems, jingles, chants, and songs as basic reading material—that is, in the enlarged print format—another naturally satisfying part of normal school experience could be turned directly to literacy learning.

Security and joy developed naturally for both children and teacher. Favorite books soon carried with them all the secure associations of an old friend; children began going to books to *achieve* security. Because of the high impact of the books, and the teacher's pleasure-sharing role, joy was a common experience for all the children.

As for the teachers themselves, because they were doing something at the center of their competence rather than attempting to follow a half-understood methodology, they too, experienced security and joy. They were able to develop their skill in using the natural opportunities for teaching gradually from a confident base—if attention were lost or a teaching point fell flat, they simply stepped back into the story, got it moving again, and recaptured the interest of the children.

Furthermore, they were able to engage in the input, reading activity with the whole class or a large group without a sense of guilt. (Try reading a captivating story to one group while the others carry out group tasks within earshot!) The problem of matching children to appropriate materials, or of keeping a group going at the same pace so as not to end up with nine or ten groups, almost disappeared. It was now the responsibility of each learner to select the materials he or she would "work on." Even though the teachers were using a new methodology with unusual priorities, their sense of relief from the pressures of structured programs and their enjoyment of the language period grew rapidly.

Once the decision had been made to put other priorities

aside in an attempt to establish this model as the central framework of the reading program, the practical application proved a remarkably simple matter. The task now was to refine the procedures in the light of professional knowledge from many sources in order to get optimal educational returns from the simple learning structure which had been set up.

A typical teaching-learning sequence of shared book experience in many classrooms developed along the following lines:

Opening warm-up	Favorite poems, jingles, songs, with enlarged text. Teaching of new poem or song.
Old favorite	Enjoyment of a favorite sotry in enlarged format. Teaching of skills in context. Deepening understanding. Unison participation. Role playing, dramatization.
Language games, especially alphabet	Alphabet games, rhymes, and songs, using letter names. Fun with words and sounds, meaningful situations. (Not isolated phonic drills.)
New story	Highlight of session. Long story may be broken naturally into two or more parts. Inducing word-solving strategies in context, participation in prediction and confirmation of new vocabulary.
Output activities	Independent reading from wide selection of favorites. Related arts activities stemming from new story. Creative writing often using structures from new story. Playing teacher—several children enjoy favorite together—one acting as teacher.

Development of shared book experience techniques went on for several years in key schools. Because the procedures tended to be communicated through demonstration and discussion, documentation was regrettably limited during this time. As a result of local and national in-service courses, and observation by hundreds of teachers and students in these key schools, the ideas spread rapidly. They tended to be used to supplement current procedures, and many mixed styles of teaching arose.

In 1973, convinced that the ideas deserved careful trial, the Department of Education nominated a large experimental school in a new housing area for the trial of these and other approaches. It was important to determine that shared book experience procedures could lead to effective literacy without the support of other programs or materials, and so one class of 35 beginners was taught for two years by these procedures alone. No graded or structured materials were used and all word-solving skills were taught in context during real reading. This experimental group proved equal or superior to other experimental and control groups on a variety of measures including Marie Clay's *Diagnostic Survey* (1980). Of greatest significance was the highly positive attitudes toward reading displayed by the slow-developing children after two years in the natural, shared book experience environment.

Following this study, the Department of Education embarked on an ambitious, national in-service program for primary teachers which was known as the "Early Reading In-service Course," and a complementary program for parents in both radio and print media (Horton 1978). The radical movement of early schooling toward developmental models has been accomplished on a national scale, albeit the scale of a small nation.

Much has been done internationally since then, and more remains to be done. From our own symposium Yetta Goodman (1980), Margaret Meek (1982), and Dorothy Butler (1979 and 1980) have contributed to that growing movement in literacy toward plain, human, good sense. The pioneering figures, Goodman (e.g., 1968, 1979), Frank Smith (e.g., 1978), and Marie Clay (e.g., 1980), have continued to inform the movement. Recent work in writing, such as is brought together in Temple et al. (1982), extends insights over the full corpus of literacy. Practical professionals, such as Robert and Marlene McCracken (1979), Mark Aulis (1982), Anne Pulvertaft (1978), and F. L. Barrett (1982) in their diverse ways support teachers in the daily enterprise of application. Researchers too numerous to list, among them David Doake, Judith Newman, Elizabeth Sulzby, and Robert Teale, push back the frontiers.

Space does not permit a discussion of the written language and related arts aspects of shared book experience programs. When children are motivated to express themselves under the influence of a rich and highly familiar literature, and when such facilitating conditions for expression are provided, the outcomes are extremely satisfying. The whole set of ideas, sometimes referred to now as "holistic," is complex, rich, and compelling. Certainly it promises us a clarity beyond eclecticism and an opportunity to use our own deep responses to what is memorable in print toward the mastery of literacy within the environment of early schooling.

CONCLUDING REMARKS

This [chapter] has attempted to describe a complex movement of research and development spread over some 15 years and involving professional contributions too numerous and too subtle to be fully analyzed. There is an obvious need for specific research of many kinds within this framework. The purpose of this [chapter] has been to bring together a set of ideas which both challenges some of our most sacred instructional assumptions and points to alternative models as appropriate and eminently workable.

The acquisition of spoken language in infancy is a highly complex process, but there are a number of very simple and natural insights at the center of our success in providing favorable conditions for the process to be learned. Experience and research suggest that a very similar set of simple and natural insights facilitate the mastery of literacy skills. Among these is that we may provide favorable conditions for learning literacy tasks in developmental ways such as using children's favorite books, and the powerful strategies they induce, at the very center of the literacy program.

Chapter 7

MODELED WRITING: REFLECTIONS ON THE CONSTRUCTIVE PROCESS

by Maryann Manning and Gary Manning, University of Alabama at Birmingham

The authors take the reader into the classrooms of two teachers to analyze children's construction of knowledge during modeled writing. They describe what teachers do in modeled writing and give examples of individual children's statements in specific situations.

The authors' reason for reporting children's remarks is that these statements are manifestations of the constructive process. For example, if the teacher is writing "the," and a child announces that Texas *is spelled with a big* T, *we can infer that this child is thinking about the letter* t *and the conditions under which it has to be capitalized. It is by thinking (making relationships) that children construct knowledge, rather than by memorizing rules. The chapter shows that different children construct different aspects of literacy during modeled writing.*

"That means she's done," Jimmy whispered to Marcus as they watched their teacher, Leigh Martin, put a period at the end of a sentence. The two boys were watching her write on a large piece of paper. With the other first graders sitting on the floor close to Mrs. Martin, Marcus whispered back, "If she don't put that, she has to write more."

First graders in whole-language classrooms watch their

111

teachers write every day. The modeled writing that they watch results in learning from the inside as evidenced by Jimmy and Marcus's statements. Children do not spontaneously talk about things in which they are not interested. We can therefore say that the two boys were expressing interest in how periods are used. This interest from within is essential for the construction of knowledge.

The children love to watch Mrs. Martin write. They enjoy trying to figure out what she is writing and talking with her and one another about what has been written. As children watch their teachers, parents, and others write, they try to make sense of the writer's behavior.

The roots of modern-day modeled writing can be found in the language experience approach as described by Roach Van Allen. He advocated group language experience in which the teacher takes dictation from the children, writing down their words exactly as dictated. Many language experience teachers focused on the idea that writing is talk written down, and children's oral language became a major part of the written language they read. Whole-language teachers in New Zealand, Australia, Canada, and the United States have further developed the practice of taking dictation. These teachers have new understandings about written language and realize that written language has forms and functions that are not necessarily the same as those of oral language. Thus, teachers using modeled writing do not merely take dictation. The children do not always know in advance the content of the text; they usually have to figure it out by reading as the teacher writes and/or by talking with the teacher and each other.

During modeled writing, the teacher writes slowly thinking aloud about the content and the mechanics. She may say, for example, "Should I put a period here?" The teacher sits close to the children for better communication and a feeling of community. She writes on a chalkboard or a large sheet of paper attached to an easel. She sometimes asks for children's opinions about words to use, how to spell them, and about mechanics. The teacher makes sure that the content is interesting and meaningful for the students. The source of the content varies; the teacher uses her/his own ideas on some days while on other days the ideas come directly from the children. The complexity of the writing and the involvement of the children depend on the ages and literacy levels of the children.

After the text has been written, the teacher and the children read it together several times. The text is then displayed in the classroom for reference and rereading.

Children watch the teacher write words and sentences. They observe the thinking processes of a writer as the teacher verbalizes thoughts such as, "Will this make sense to my readers?" They see that what is written can be read. They construct ideas about written language as can be seen in the following examples.

Although Mrs. Martin usually does not announce the subject of the text, she said on this particular day that she was going to write about her cat. She then wrote the following lines on a large sheet of paper.

My Hungry Cat

My cat looks at me through the window. He makes noises so I will feed him. I wonder how long he waits for me in the morning. How does your pet ask for food?

Leigh does modeled writing every day and the children know they can talk quietly to each other as they watch her write and try to read the text. Two of the children were looking around the room and not at the text. One little boy got up in the middle of the writing, went to his seat, and sat quietly until the end of the activity. If some children are not interested in modeled writing at a particular point, they find something else to do that is of interest. This freedom differs greatly from a traditional class-room, where children are forced to participate in predetermined activities that may make no sense to them. Leigh continued to write and occasionally asked for children's opinions and advice. When she began to write the word *window*, she wrote *w* and asked, "What other letters do I need?" One child said, "A *d* because it makes the *d* sound."

After writing a capital *H* in *He* at the beginning of the second sentence, the teacher asked, "Why did I write a big *H*?" One child answered, "The first word always has a big one."

When she wrote *feed* in the second sentence, one child declared, "It has a *s* on it." Another child who had been silent announced, "You don't say *feeds*, it don't make sense. I will *feed* him." The child who wanted the *s* did not say anything but nodded as if in agreement.

Leigh asked for help with the spelling of *waits*. She wrote in the margins the different spellings as the children gave them: *was, watz,* and *wats.* One little boy went across the room to get the dictionary and suggested, "Look it up in the dictionary." Children construct different ideas as they experience modeled writing because they bring different kinds and amounts of knowledge to the situation. However, as Kamii suggests in Chapter 1, a child who has the possibility of hearing English is more likely to construct the English language than one who is not exposed to it. Likewise, children who observe their teacher write regularly are more likely to construct knowledge about written English, especially if they talk about writing with the teacher and other children.

One little girl who could not read the text was eager to know what was being written; whenever Leigh finished a line, she loudly requested, "Read it!" Leigh went on to finish the text and read it aloud as she pointed to each word. The same little girl was so interested in the text that she said the words over and over as if she wanted to make them her own.

Leigh has several children who do not always know words as separate units. For example, during independent writing time, Susan had written "mimamgtausdcr" for *My mama got a used car.*

In her modeled writing, Mrs. Martin wrote "My cat likes me" without a space between the words and asked the children if it was written correctly. Quickly a child responded, "They don't belong together, so they don't go so close." Mrs. Martin is aware of the research of Ferreiro, Sinclair and others. She realizes that, as Siegrist and Sinclair explain in Chapter 3, Susan and children at her level "introduce no blanks between words at all in short sentences." They write a sentence as one unit. Leigh knows that Susan will eventually write words as separate units in a sentence. It is pointless to correct the writing. When Susan becomes sure that "My Mama got a used car" is six words, she will write them as six words without being told.

In modeled writing, children construct their own understandings of written language, and each child constructs something different. Realizing the developmental nature of children's learning, Leigh responds differently to children at different levels. Below are some other aspects of writing and reading that we have observed during modeled writing sessions in Leigh Martin's classroom and in the classroom of another whole-language teacher, Cinna Sotherland.

GRAPHOPHONIC INFORMATION

Children watch teachers using different letters during modeled writing. Leigh asked her children one day how they thought *oxygen* was spelled. She had four different responses, "oxjgen," "oxigen," "oxegen," and "osxgen." All four spellings indicate much knowledge about graphophonics. Leigh values social interaction realizing that children make new relationships about how words are spelled as they consider other children's ideas about spelling. The children voted on what they considered to be the best way to spell *oxygen*. They decided that it was spelled *oxigen*.

Children in Leigh's class are at different developmental levels. For instance, Sam has not constructed the sound-symbol correspondences, and is aware only of the names of some letters. During one modeled writing session, Leigh asked for help in spelling *hungry*. John, an advanced reader and writer, volunteered, "It ends with *y*. I know it's a *y* even if it isn't giving a *ya* sound but an *e* sound." When children and the teacher offer ideas about different graphophonic aspects, other children like Sam often make new graphophonic relationships.

CAPITALIZATION

When Leigh wrote *the,* Keyton stood up and exclaimed: "If you write *Texas,* you need a big letter even if it isn't at the first." Since *the* and *Texas* both begin with a *t,* Keyton thought about *Texas* when he saw Mrs. Martin write *the.* He seemed to be trying to figure out why *Texas* always had a big *T* and *the* sometimes has a small *t.* Keyton did not know about common and proper nouns, but he knew that *Texas* always started with a big letter.

DIFFERENT TYPES OF WRITING

Modeled writing gives teachers an opportunity to write in different styles. Invitations, letters, recipes, expository text, expressive text, and poetry are all forms of writing that can be used in modeled writing. Within the life of a classroom, there are many opportunities to use different written forms.

We often observe in the classroom of Cinna Sotherland as she conducts modeled writing sessions with her five- and six-year-old students. On one visit, we heard her tell the students that she was going to write a different version of the story *Jack and the Bean Stalk.* As soon as Cinna sat down to begin writing, Miesha said, "Let's start with *Once upon a time.*" Because of Miesha's experience with fairy tales and expressive writing, she knew this was an appropriate way to begin. Miesha had not learned this from a lesson about story beginnings. She had constructed it by hearing many stories read by teachers and by talking with the teacher and other students about stories they were reading.

CONNECTIONS BETWEEN READING AND WRITING

During and after modeled writing, the teacher reads aloud what has been written. In classrooms of five- and six-year-olds, many children actually read as the teacher writes. When Cinna was writing "Jack took the cow to town," one little boy yelled, "t-o" as soon as the teacher had written "Jack took the cow." The child had to be able to read the first four words at some level to be able to predict that "t-o" followed them. Other children were anxious for Cinna to read the text; they wanted to know what it said.

The rereading of the modeled writing provides another opportunity for children to engage in the reading process. When Cinna's students were reading "She threw the beans away," in unison they all said, "out the window" instead of "away." Because Cinna understood that children learn to read by thinking about meaning as well as making graphophonic relationships, she did not tell them to sound out *away*. She realized that the error showed that children were making sense of what they were reading. She knew that they would eventually attend to more of the graphophonic features of the text, especially when they made errors that caused them to lose meaning as they read.

Modeled writing provides children with references for their own writing. In Leigh's and Cinna's rooms, children often go to previous writing with specific questions. For instance, Jeff, an advanced writer, did not know how to spell *happily*. He remembered that Mrs. Sotherland had used it in her writing the day before and went to the piece of paper where *happily* was written.

117

CONCLUSION

Modeled writing is a method that teachers like Leigh and Cinna use to help children construct our alphabetical writing system. However, some teachers might not use it in ways that foster children's construction of knowledge. We have seen teachers use modeled writing to "teach" isolated, predetermined skills with no regard for the developmental levels of the children involved. For example, we saw a kindergarten teacher emphasizing the letter *m* when all the children in her group were at the letter string level in which there is no letter-sound correspondence. Such teachers seem to think the purpose of modeled writing is to have children imitate and "spit out" skills.

To know what to do from one moment to the next, teachers need to be thoroughly familiar with developmental theory and research. But teachers also need to know children's personalities, developmental histories, what motivates them, and what discourages them. As Ferreiro states in Chapter 2, there is no "magic" method that will support all children's literacy development. One thing is clear, however—all children want to become competent. The teacher's task is to figure out how to use this motivation so that children will make reading and writing truly their own.

Chapter 8

READING TO KNOW

by Barbara A. Lewis and Roberta Long, University of
Alabama at Birmingham

*Lewis and Long attempted to understand why
children ask us to read certain books over and over or
read them time and again. They analyze four highly
popular books using Piaget's framework of knowledge. After analyzing them in detail, they conclude
that good books correspond well to the way in which
children construct knowledge. More specifically, the
authors say that good books are written in ways that
enable children to put (1) old bits of knowledge into
new relationships and (2) new bits of knowledge into
relationships with old knowledge.*

*Lewis and Long remind us, however, that no
two children will construct the same knowledge while
reading the same book. Children return to the same
good books perhaps because they find something
enjoyable that they can assimilate each time.*

One of the basic tenets of literacy development from a
whole-language perspective is that literature should be a
cornerstone of the instructional program. Advocates of whole
language have observed that literature, or in their words "real"
books, captures the hearts and minds of children, and in so
doing, leads them to purposeful reading and writing.

What is it about "real" books that intrigues children and
motivates them to engage in literacy activities? When we first

119

asked ourselves this question, aspects of quality literature which are generally recognized, such as appealing illustrations and interesting content, came immediately to mind. When we continued to ask what makes some illustrations appealing or content interesting, we began to examine the question from a Piagetian perspective. This led us to think about how literature functions in the child's construction of knowledge.

In Chapter 1, Kamii explains the difference between knowledge in a narrow sense and knowledge in a broad sense. An example she uses to clarify the difference between the two is the statement that Washington, D.C., is the capital of the United States. This is a specific bit of information in the narrow sense. To understand the statement, however, the child must have a framework, or knowledge in a broad sense, to know what "capital" and "the United States" are. Kamii also explains the differences among three kinds of knowledge—physical, logico-mathematical, and social knowledge—and discusses how children construct knowledge in a narrow sense as well as in a broad sense by putting elements of physical and social knowledge into relationship.

The purpose of this chapter is to illustrate the possibilities books offer for encouraging children's construction of knowledge in both a narrow and a broad sense. We analyzed four books which were recommended by teachers as ones children come back to time and time again. Any other good book, which children love, offers similar possibilities.

THE BLUE WHALE

The Blue Whale, by Donna K. Grosvenor, is a combination of narration and exposition woven around the story of a mother whale and her baby who travel together from warm waters to Antarctica and back to warmer waters again. In their journey, they meet three other kinds of whales, penguins on the icebergs of Antarctica, and whalers in boats. Many facts about whales are given. Apart from the story these facts would be dry and lifeless, but because they are contextualized, young children are fascinated by this book.

One reason for this fascination can be found in the focus on two whales with whom children can identify. The book begins with the statement "Try to imagine that you are a blue whale. You are very, very big. You are the largest animal that has ever lived." The reader's imagination is intensified by the blue-green pictures giving an underwater perspective, and children can indeed imagine gliding through the blue-green water page after page.

Another reason for the book's attraction may be the information it gives in a skillful way. Many facts dealing with specific physical knowledge about blue whales punctuate the report of their journey. One of the first things the reader finds out is that the baby whale, Big Blue, is not a fish even though he lives in the ocean.

> He is a mammal as you are, and he must breathe air.
> Instead of a nose like yours,
> he has two blowholes on the top of his head.
> Big Blue opens his blowholes above the water to get air.
> He closes them when he goes underwater.

This lesson in biology begins by making many classificatory relationships. "Fish" is a category familiar to children, but they are challenged to modify this category with the statement that the whale is not a fish. The category "mammal" is introduced next as one to which the reader belongs. The function of the blowholes is explained by analogy with the reader's nose. (An analogy consists of classificatory relationships: A nose is to a child what a blowhole is to a whale.) All these bits are specific physical knowledge about whales, but these specific bits also contribute to children's construction of knowledge in a broad sense about animals. They construct relationships among fish, whales, mammals, humans, air, and breathing.

A large part of the book deals with the spatial relationship between Antarctica and where "warmer waters" are. The reader can also make many ecological relationships as the whales continue their journey. The baby whale drinks milk from his mother's nipple, but the mother has very little to eat for six months, until she finds krill (shrimp-like animals) in Antarctica. In fact, the whole purpose of the long journey is to reach these feeding grounds. However, once there, many whales are killed to become food for humans and pets and to make oil for soap and machinery.

The book thus weaves together many elements of biology, geography, and ecology, along with bits of economics and politics. It is often said that young children's curriculum must be integrated rather than cut up into various subjects and skills. However, the truth is that young children's thinking is not differentiated yet and, therefore, there are no separate subjects for them to integrate. Children's books such as *The Blue Whale* are good for them precisely because they deal with aspects of knowledge in the broad sense as well as knowledge in the narrow sense. Facts are presented in ways that allow children to make connections with what they already know.

GRANDMAMA'S JOY

Grandmama's Joy, by Eloise Greenfield, is a fictional story about a little girl named Rhondy and her grandmother. The interactions between the two take place during one afternoon, but their feelings and memories, the main subject of the book, encompass a period going back to the time before Rhondy's birth.

> Her grandmama was sad and Rhondy didn't know why. It wasn't one of those rainy, gray days that sometimes made grandmama so quiet. It was a gold and blue day.

Rhondy tries to make her grandmama laugh by putting on a show. Grandmama laughs and claps at Rhondy's performance, but Rhondy can tell from the lines between Grandmama's eyes that she is still sad. After Rhondy gives Grandmama a pretty black stone with silvery speckles she finds in the yard, Grandmama begins to cry. Finally, Grandmama explains that they have to leave their yard and house. She can no longer afford the rent.

At this point, there is a temporal shift in the story as Grandmama tells Rhondy that she has lived in that house since before Rhondy's birth. Rhondy asks her to tell her the story about when she came to live with her. Grandmama is reluctant so Rhondy begins: "It was a rainy, gray day . . ." Once more, Grandmama tells Rhondy that when she was just a little baby the car in which she was riding with her parents crashed into a tree. When Grandmama found Rhondy at the hospital, she picked her up and declared, "That's my joy, that's Grandmama's joy. Long as I got my joy, I'll be all right." "Am I still your joy?" Rhondy asks. And, then, reminding her grandmama of what they will always have because they are together, Rhondy continues, "Will I still be your joy when we move?"

This is a poignant, powerful story for children because most wonder if their parents' love will be constant as they and events in their lives change. To understand this book, children must put many events into temporal relationships. The book also includes many bits of social knowledge which young children may or may not understand (rent, money, and another dwelling where the rent is lower). Its main focus, however, is not on content but on Rhondy's thinking, or the relationships she makes. From the specific bits of physical facts Rhondy observed, she made inferences about her grandmother's internal state. Children categorize genuine laughs and forced pretense, as well as focused gazes and faraway looks, and *know* when emotional responses are not sincere.

Books such as *Grandmama's Joy* give children a chance to

react to a much wider spectrum of human feelings and relationships than they might ordinarily encounter in their daily lives. In the context of the story, children can confirm or reassess their predictions related to motives and behavior and the consequences of certain actions. Books provide a safe place for children to test and elaborate their knowledge and feelings as they enter the lives of the characters they meet.

A HOUSE IS A HOUSE FOR ME

Mary Ann Hoberman's *A House Is a House for Me* is a book of poems and relationships that is hard to classify. It begins with the following three lines illustrated with lively pictures of ants on a hill, bees near a beehive, and playful mice:

A hill is a house for an ant, an ant.
A hive is a house for a bee.
A hole is a house for a mole or a mouse . . .

Upon turning the page, we find the picture of a young child in a tree house reading books, and the refrain "And a house is a house for me."

After several similar pages about a house for a spider, a bird, a bug, a chick, a cow, and a dog, the reader comes to anthropological and cultural contents. A "house" as a shelter is described for trains and planes, corn and peas, and hands and knees. The reader realizes, with Hoberman, that the more "I think about houses, the more things are houses for things."

A "house" eventually changes its meaning and becomes a container:

A teapot's a house for some tea.
If you pour me a cup and I drink it all up,
Then the teahouse will turn into me!

This book presents a host of relationships and a new perspective for old relationships involving the category "house."

Through the use of metaphors and clever pictures, it gives children opportunities to elaborate their knowledge in a broad sense. Within this framework, it also gives many specific bits of knowledge in a narrow sense such as the fact that turtles have shells as do oysters, lobsters, and clams.

PEOPLE

People, written and illustrated by Peter Spier, highlights the many ways in which people are the same and different. The first page contains mathematics, geography, and astronomy and begins by telling the reader that no two persons in the world are exactly the same:

> By the year 2000 there will be 6,000,000,000 people on earth. If we all joined hands, the line would be 3,805,871 miles long and would stretch 153 times around the equator. Or sixteen times the distance to the moon. More than 4,000,000,000 people . . . and no two of them alike!

The book focuses first on physical knowledge and shows through numerous illustrations how aspects of the human body—sizes and shapes, skin colors, eyes, noses, and hair—can be different. The focus then shifts to social knowledge, and there is one page each showing people wearing all kinds of clothes, living in all kinds of houses, eating or avoiding different foods, playing in a variety of ways, and practicing different religions. Many pages are also devoted to values such as beauty. One illustration shows various ways in which people the world over adorn themselves. The reader finds out that while a particular adornment may be considered beautiful in one culture, it may be "considered ugly, or even ridiculous, elsewhere."

Social differences among people, as well as physical, cultural, and geographical, are also addressed. On one page, for example, the contrast is shown between a well-maintained suburban area and a deteriorated, poverty-ridden one. The illustrations and text convey the fact that many people in the world are wretchedly poor even though some are not. On yet another page, illustrations of people with power, such as a military commander and a corporate executive, are placed above a picture of a mass of people moving through a train station. We read that "Some people, but very few, are mighty and powerful, although most of us are not mighty at all."

This book categorizes people in at least 28 different ways and shows the surprisingly large number of ways in which people are alike and different. Children can study the numerous detailed, and often humorous, pictures that give specific bits of knowledge within a meaningful context and find new ways of "seeing" the world around them.

CONCLUSION

We began this chapter by asking why children are intrigued by certain books and are motivated to read them again and again. As we saw in the preceding analysis of four books, one explanation may be that well-written books present facts and concepts in ways that allow children to elaborate their knowledge in both a narrow and a broad sense. All children want to make sense of the world, and well-written books meet this need in two ways: by letting children put (1) old bits of knowledge into new relationships, and (2) new bits of knowledge into relationship with old knowledge. An example of this is a child who has some understanding of mammals and the physical characteristics of whales before participating in the shared reading of *The Blue Whale*. For this child, the time may be right to find out that a whale (old knowledge) is not a fish but a mammal (new relationship). In addition, finding out that whales might become extinct because they are hunted for meat and oil (new knowledge) may allow a child to put whales into a new relationship with human beings.

It is important to remember that no two children will construct the same knowledge upon reading or participating in the shared reading of a book. Each child will get something different from the same book because each brings different prior knowledge to the situation.

While teachers cannot know or predetermine the outcomes a certain book will elicit, they can do several things to maximize children's construction of knowledge. After selecting a book that is inherently interesting, the teacher needs to read it well with enthusiasm and ask intriguing questions along the way. After reading, it is important to encourage the exchange of points of view among children. The rest is up to the children. When children go back to a particular book many times, the teacher can tell that there is something in the book that satisfies their needs and interests.

Chapter 9

AN APPROACH TO ASSESSMENT IN EARLY LITERACY

by Brenda S. Engel, Lesley College Graduate School, Cambridge, Massachusetts

Engel suggests specific procedures for assessing young children's literacy in ways that are consistent with developmental theory. Referring to many parents' use of baby books to "keep track" of their children's development, she suggests that educators, too, "keep track" of children's literacy development in a similar way. She argues that by using descriptive assessment procedures, teachers can record milestones of what happens, when and how. This is a much more informative approach than achievement tests, which compare children's performance on superficial skills on one specific day.

If educators followed the principles and procedures suggested by Engel, assessment would encourage teachers to move toward whole-language practices. Unfortunately, today, achievement tests are influencing them to use drill sheets containing test-like items. Drilling children to do well on tests does not result in their reading critically or writing clearly.

This chapter appeared in Achievement Testing in the Early Grades: The Games Grown-Ups Play, *edited by Constance Kamii (Washington, D.C.: National Association for the Education of*

Young Children, 1990, pp. 119–34). Reprinted with permission.

According to the common wisdom, children learn to read when they get to school, except those few, like John Stuart Mill, whose parents teach them at home at age 2 or 3, or like Heidi, who simply teach themselves. Progressive educators, however, have long understood reading and writing as developmental, beginning virtually at birth. Over the past two decades, a body of international research has reinforced this view of literacy learning. (See work by Smith 1971; Clay 1979; Holdaway 1979; Ferreiro and Teberosky 1982; Graves 1982; Harste, Woodward, and Burke 1984; and Goodman 1986, among others.) Reading and writing, along with speaking and listening, are understood as facets of language learning, and reading itself is increasingly understood as the ability to get meaning from print (rather than the ability to decode print into sound). This new conception necessitates new approaches to assessment.

It is not an exaggeration to say that acquisition of language, that uniquely human and almost magical capability, begins at birth with the infant's response to voice. By the time children get to school, whether to preschool or kindergarten, they already know an uncanny amount about oral and written language: They can speak and understand complex sentences and know that print usually represents words; they can probably read some words (like "STOP" or "Corn Chex") and write a few letters (like X and O); they may also know about beginnings and endings (like "Once upon a time ..." and "The End").

Most middle-class children know that newspapers and fairy tales differ in tone; that menus, phone books, and shopping lists are not composed of sentences; that puns are funny; and that, no matter how hard they try, they won't be able to teach a dog to talk. Children from less privileged backgrounds, too, have acquired a good deal of this kind of knowledge before school.

Given a reasonably positive school situation, children will

go right on learning about language. Sometime in the early elementary grades, most become able to get meaning from unfamiliar texts without help. Most also learn to write conventionally enough so that others can read their compositions. My point is that, under favorable conditions, literacy, as an aspect of language learning, develops from birth on in an ever-expanding, uninterrupted continuum; it is driven by the child's own impulse toward competence and participation in the world's events.

KEEPING TRACK IS ONE WAY TO EVALUATE PROGRESS

Evaluation as "keeping track" begins at birth and continues into the school years. Parents and caretakers are likely to note a baby's first words: "baa" (for "bottle") or "gaga" (for "doggie"), sometimes even recording such milestones in a baby book. They might note when an infant first tries to put together two words or, later on, might save a child's simulation of a shopping list or crude attempt to form the letters in her own name.

"Keeping track" in this manner constitutes a kind of evaluation. Because ordinary development is both expected and celebrated, the overall tone is positive and confirming. There is always, of course, a slight possibility that ordinary development won't occur—that something may be wrong—so early home-style evaluation acts as reassurance of expected progress.

There are several reasons why "keeping track" seems a desirable way to approach evaluation of early literacy learning, at least through second grade:

- It meets the need for accountability while preserving the recognition and encouragement that have successfully supported growth and change before schooling.
- It is based on an assumption of success, not failure; is primarily descriptive rather than judgmental; and is

not norm referenced.

- It provides an account of what happens, when, and how, rather than what should happen.

When parents keep track of infants' learning, they themselves are the monitors, not responsible to anyone beyond possibly a grandparent or two. The moment a child enters school, however, the responsibility for keeping track shifts: Virtually everyone has a vested interest in school children's learning, from the children and their families to teachers, administrators, school board members, and the larger community of taxpayers.

The problem becomes, then, how to provide adequate information to each of these constituencies, but preserve the usefulness and positive quality of the before-school kind of evaluation. The problem is complicated by the fact that different constituencies need different kinds of information in different forms: Children need to know that they're making progress and that their abilities and special qualities are appreciated; parents (or caretakers) need more specific information and reassurance about children's progress; teachers need information on how and what children are learning to use as feedback for teaching; administrators and community members need to know, in summary form, the progress children are making.

A possible solution to the problem of the different needs of various constituencies is to organize evaluation information on three levels:

1. raw descriptive data about individual children,
2. summaries and interpretations of the raw data about individual children, and
3. quantified information about groups.

On the following pages, I suggest some possible contents for these three levels without attempting to provide recipes or comprehensive programs for assessment.

LEVEL ONE: PRIMARY DATA

This collection of data—literacy interviews, reading tapes, and teacher observations—should meet the needs of teachers and children and, to some extent, parents.

Literacy Folders

Collections of children's work are the principal means of keeping track; individual folders containing periodic, dated samples of drawings, other artwork, and writing (including ideas; plans; lists of books, stories, and poems read). The contents of the folders should be systematic, up-to-date, and available for review by teachers, children, and, during conferences, parents. Samples of children's uncorrected writing (that is, with the original "invented spelling") on child-selected subjects are of particular interest. The samples convey the history and quality of a child's involvement in literacy learning.

The most important advantage of this kind of evidence is its undoubted authenticity. The children's work stands for itself, proves its own point. Learning, rather than being claimed or expressed in percentiles or grade levels, is made visible. Direct evidence is both interesting and significant because it conveys quality, the element that is lost as information is abstracted, quantified, and prepared for a wider audience. Actual examples retain the recognizable idiosyncratic character of the particular child as well as the characteristics the child has in common with all other children.

Literacy Interviews

I have used audiotape recordings to keep track of children's progress into literacy from preschool into the primary grades. For preschoolers or children who are "emergent readers," the taping sessions take the form of "literacy interviews." I ask the child to choose a favorite book. We then settle down together in a relatively secluded corner of the classroom to "read" the book. I turn on the tape recorder and begin with some questions:

"Can you tell me where the front of the book is?" "What is this book about?" "Can you put your finger on where the story begins?"

I encourage the child to tell me the story as we turn the pages, or, if it seems indicated, I read the story aloud, stopping frequently so the child can guess at a word or anticipate what is about to happen. We look at the pictures as well as the print.

The occasion is meant to be relaxed and friendly. I do, however, have an agenda: to assess where the child is on the developmental continuum in respect to reading and what his or her feelings are about books. Specifically, I'm curious about whether the child likes the book, has a sense of story and can paraphrase the text, "gets the point," understands directionality (left-right, up-down), knows the significance of any punctuation marks, recognizes any letters or words, and understands the relationship of lower and upper case letters. I ask the child also about other favorite books, whether there are books available at home, whether she is read to at home and how often, and how much television she watches.

The interview is relatively short—about 10 minutes— and I make a few descriptive notes as well as recording the session. I label the tape (preferably the 60-minute kind) with the child's name and the date of the interview. The next interview or oral reading, also dated, is put on the same tape, beginning where the previous one left off. The inventory (described in Level Two) can be used to record information from the interview in a more formal way. (If the teacher conducts interviews in the classroom, she may have to do them in bits and pieces; tape recording may not be possible at all and the teacher's notes will then constitute the record.)

Oral Reading Tapes

Children who are beginning to read on their own can be recorded reading a story at an appropriate level of difficulty (i.e., not too hard and not too easy). Show the child a selection of stories, reading the titles and giving some idea of what each story is about. The child then selects an appropriate one to read aloud into the tape recorder. (Most second graders and some first graders can, with clear instructions, record themselves.) Afterward, ask the child, "Can you tell me what the story was about?" ("retelling").

Oral reading tapes provide excellent records of children's development in reading. A teacher or parent will find it more informative and interesting to listen to a tape of a child reading a story than to review reading scores. Children themselves are endlessly interested in their own work and recorded history, particularly as they are reminded of their youngest selves and see evidence of growth and change.

Although the collection of tapes for a whole class will be useful to mark the progress of individuals and the group, some can be selectively scored—not necessarily for *all* children, but for those children for whom more detailed information might be useful. The method of scoring, shown in Table 9.1, is a modified version of miscue analysis (Goodman 1979). It may, at first, seem complicated and time consuming. However, it soon becomes fairly automatic: A teacher experienced in the method can score a tape, using the Oral Reading Appraisal Form shown in Figure 9.1, in about 10 to 30 minutes, depending on the length of the text read.

The accuracy score is important only as baseline information on the appropriateness of the text level. If literal word-by-word accuracy is below 95 percent, the child is likely to flounder and lose ability to use strategies he would ordinarily have at his disposal. If the accuracy rate is 100, the child could probably handle a more difficult text.

135

Table 9.1
Procedures for Scoring Oral Reading Tapes*

1. *Marking text:* Use photocopy of text read.
   - Listen to tape, underlining all mistakes (where spoken word differs from printed one). Optional: Write above printed word what reader actually said, when it differed from text. Don't count the same mistake twice.
   - Indicate self-corrections by putting "C" above word corrected.
   - Circle any words omitted.
   - Put caret (^) in space if extra word is added, writing in extra word above.
   - If letters or words are reversed, mark with horizontal S (ᘔ).
   - Make notes on retelling (comprehension, completeness) and on particular qualities of reading (fluency, expressiveness, nature of mistakes, etc.).

2. *Preparing to score reading:*
   - Count and note total number of words in text.
   - Go through text, putting slash (/) in margin opposite each mistake.
   - Go through text a second time and put line through slashes (X) where mistakes have not been corrected (no "C" above word) or if it is not "supportive of meaning" (i.e., if it destroys syntax or meaning). For example, if the child reads, "It was a nice house" instead of "It was a nice home," the word "house" counts as a meaningful mistake and you don't cross out the slash. But if the child reads, "It was a nice harm," the mistake destroys meaning, and you should put a cross through the slash: X.

3. *Scoring:*
   - Accuracy rate: total number of words minus number of mistakes plus self-corretions divided by the total number of words.

$$\frac{\text{words} - \text{mistakes} + \text{self-corrections}}{\text{total words}}$$

*For use with Oral Reading Appraisal Form (Figure 9.1).

Table 9.1 (Continued)

- Meaningful mistake rate: total number of single slashes divided by total number of single and crossed slashes.

$$\frac{\text{total /}}{\text{total / + X}}$$

- Self-correction rate: total number of self-corrections divided by total number of single and crossed slashes.

$$\frac{\text{total self-corrections}}{\text{total / + X}}$$

- Comprehension or retelling score:
  1 = fragmentary understanding
  2 = partial understanding
  3 = fairly complete understanding
  4 = full and complete understanding

- Text level: Use either publisher's text level equivalent or estimate level based on comparison with those of published texts. Levels do not represent grade levels; they are the publisher's arbitrary numbering of texts.

Figure 9.1
Oral Reading Appraisal Form

Student ————————————— Date of birth —————————

Grade ———————— Teacher ————————— School —————————

Date of reading ————————————— Favorite book read —————————

Name of text read ————————————— Level of text —————————

Accuracy rate:

$$\frac{\text{total words} - \text{total mistakes} + \text{total self-corrections}}{\text{total words}}$$

$$= \underline{\hspace{4cm}}$$

Meaningful mistakes rate:

$$\frac{\text{meaningful mistakes}}{\text{total mistakes}}$$

$$= \underline{\hspace{4cm}}$$

Self-correction rate:

$$\frac{\text{self-corrections}}{\text{total mistakes}}$$

$$= \underline{\hspace{4cm}}$$

Comments:

Both the meaningful mistake rate and the self-correction rate assess the child's determination to have the text make sense. In general, the higher the percentage, the more the child can be said to be reading for meaning. (If a child reads with near 100% accuracy, however, these percentages will have less significance, since there will be less opportunity for constructive mistakes or self-corrections.)

Teacher Observations

Teachers are the best sources of descriptive data on children. They know individual children well and are likely to be present at significant moments—moments of visible learning. Teachers too can use their observations to inform teaching. Note taking, however, can be difficult in a demanding classroom situation. A few suggestions may help:

- Focus on one child as much as possible for one day.
- Keep on hand a roll of gummed labels on which to write brief observational notes at moments during the day. At the end of the day, date labels and stick them on the inside cover of the child's folder.
- Make both language and content as descriptive as possible.
- Avoid making ambitious plans or setting schedules that will be hard to maintain; consistency is more important than frequency.

The following observation was made by a kindergarten teacher in an urban public school:

When he was finished with his journal picture, he surprised me by suddenly starting to write various letters on his page: P for Philip and then said E for Eliza (later also said Z for Eliza!), B for Binyamin. I had no idea that he knew all those letters, much less that he associated them correctly with names.

A continuous collection of primary data is, like the baby book, descriptive, affirming, and relevant, a rich mine of sequential material that embodies learning and can inform teaching. It is also unwieldy, however, and at some point it calls for review and interpretation—which brings me to the second level of evaluation.

LEVEL TWO: SUMMARIES OF INDIVIDUAL CHILDREN'S PROGRESS

This second level of evaluation, still a way of "keeping track," interprets and summarizes the primary data. It includes teacher notes and comments, inventories, and analyses of oral reading tapes. No new information is added.

Teacher Notes and Comments

Teachers should review each child's literacy folder periodically, adding at this time to their own descriptive notes and making further comments on breakthroughs in understanding, interests, progress in mastering conventions, expressiveness, and so on. Such reviews can be in preparation for parents conferences, for year-end reports, or simply for routine record-keeping scheduled regularly throughout the school year.

The following example is excerpted from an anecdotal year-end report to parents of a kindergarten child.

Of all the children in the class, P has probably made the most spectacular progress this year! One of the youngest, fully a year younger than the oldest child, P entered the class without separation problems but appeared bewildered and withdrawn. He didn't know how to store the blocks by size, he couldn't count his crackers correctly, and he didn't speak.

By the late fall, P started to get more involved with materials in the classroom. He also became much more social and began to imitate some of the activities of the other children,

140

particularly counting and sorting games. His oral language developed dramatically at this point. P's pattern seems to be to observe for a long time and take everything in quietly. Then, when he feels confident, he tries out a new activity for himself.

Literacy Inventories

Inventories are summaries of children's literacy learning. Completed on the basis of the primary data, they are useful ways of "taking stock." An example is shown in Figure 9.2.

Inventories are not to be confused with check lists or scope-and-sequence charts. Unlike a check list, an inventory has meaning in terms of the overall picture: No single item represents a necessary achievement. Also, *unlike check lists and scope-and-sequence charts, which are set out ahead of the child pointing the way, inventories follow or "keep track of" what has already happened. This distinction is important: It concerns the difference between prescription and description. We are describing what is—in other words, "keeping track"—not prescribing what should be.* The procedures detailed in this chapter all depend on description and assume, as I stated at the beginning, that literacy learning for children is a natural extension of language development.

Oral Reading Tapes

The procedures involved in taping oral reading samples have already been outlined. The scoring procedures are shown in Table 9.1.

Figure 9.2
Descriptive Inventory

	yes	possibly	not yet
1. Enjoys books and stories			
2. Seeks book experiences, asks for or goes to books spontaneously			
3. Is curious about print			
4. Experiments with written language			
5. Is able to follow plot, sequences			
6. Can predict words, phrases			
7. Knows story comes from print			
8. Will tell story of familiar text, turning pages			
9. Knows directional conventions: left-right, top-bottom			
10. Understands print entities: words, letters			
11. Understands phonetic principle: letters related to speech sounds			
12. Understands consistency principle: same word is spelled the same way			
13. Knows 12 or more letter sounds			
14. Tries invented spelling			
15. Approximates reading with familiar text			
16. Recognizes 12 or more words			
17. Can sound out some words			
18. Knows two or more conventions of punctuation			

LEVEL THREE: QUANTIFIED INFORMATION ABOUT GROUPS

The third level of evaluation, which includes class summaries, statistics, and graphs, is designed for administrators and the public. With the exception of class summaries, this quantified information will hold less interest for teachers, children, and parents. The information, which should be assembled by administrative personnel (i.e., not by teachers), is abstracted from the primary data, some of it by way of the interpreted dat[a] in Level Two of evaluation. No new instruments or information are added except, perhaps, routine school and school department statistics.

Class Summaries

Class summaries, in anecdotal form, are useful for school administrators (who can, in turn, further condense the information for central office records) in order to "flag" children who might be in need of attention. Following is an example of such a summary of a first grade class (names have been changed):

Twenty-nine children (in two classes) were recorded reading aloud: 18 boys and 11 girls. Six children, about a fifth of the class, were still "emergent readers," not able to make sense of an unfamiliar text: Kendall Arthur, Marian Jasper, Robert Merriam, Robert Aventino, Jonathan Tinbergen, and Katherine Rantulli. Katherine Rantulli had been retained from the previous year. This is about the expected proportion, roughly the same as in previous years. The average text level read with over 95 percent accuracy was level 6, up two levels from the previous year's first grade. (Levels do not represent grade levels but rather publishers' arbitrary numbering of texts).

The following seven students, although able to "decode" a text with fair word-by-word accuracy, were not able to retell the content with much detail: Colin Cameron, David Santiago, Donna Judson, Barbara Jordan, Hasan Said, Leo Albion, and Uri David.

On the whole, children who had been in the school the previous year, in kindergarten, were reading on a slightly higher level and with better comprehension, more self-correction, and more demand for meaning. Word-by-word accuracy rates were about the same as that of the new children.

Statistics

Information about reading levels (from tape recordings) and results of literacy inventories can be summarized in numerical tables. An example is shown in Table 9.2. Writing, an equally important aspect of literacy learning, is, like other art forms, not easily amenable to quantitative representation. We have kept records of word and sentence counts but have not yet developed a very satisfactory way of summarizing quality.

Graphs

Reading levels can be effectively presented in graphic form. Figure 9.3 shows reading levels of 10 children grades 2 to 4. Kept over time, graphs like this one will effectively illustrate progress. A similar graph can be made with class averages over three (or more) years.

FEASIBILITY

Because of differences among schools in resources, available personnel, teachers' schedules and responsibilities, and class sizes, it is possible here to make only modest suggestions for helping "keeping track" become classroom reality:

1. Enlist children's participation, particularly in collecting and dating work samples and tape-recording oral reading.
2. Build data collection into the instructional program, scheduling activities at regular intervals for the academic year.

Table 9.2
Oral Reading Score of 10 Children
for 1987 and 1988

Child	Oral Reading Score for 1987				
	Accuracy ratio (%)	Meaningful mistake ratio (%)	Self-correction ratio (%)	Comprehension estimate	Text level
1	97	50	33	4	2
2	96	29	10	3	3
3	*	*	*	*	*
4	90	21	18	2	2
5	94	33	15	3	4
6	92	53	25	3	4
7	96	50	26	4	5
8	95	38	10	4	2
9	99	50	30	2	2
10	98	71	40	4	3

Child	Oral Reading Score for 1988				
	Accuracy ratio (%)	Meaningful mistake ratio (%)	Self-correction ratio (%)	Comprehension estimate	Text level
1	*	*	*	*	*
2	96	59	27	2	6
3	93	50	27	4	4
4	97	64	30	4	8
5	96	77	22	3	10
6	95	63	10	3	7
7	95	80	13	3	8
8	95	85	42	4	5
9	98	36	45	3	7
10	98	100	50	4	8

Note: Text level is the publisher's rating. It does not denote a grade.
* = not tested

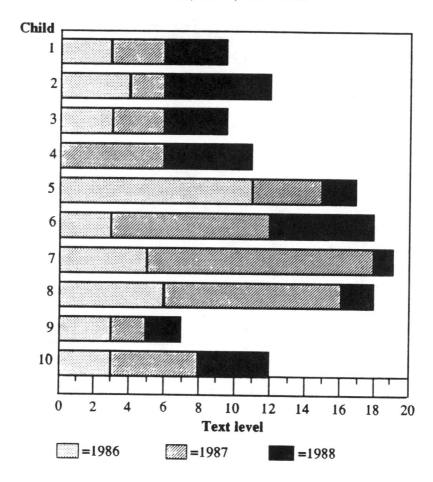

Figure 9.3
Oral Reading Levels of 10 Children
for 1986, 1987, and 1988

3. Use any help you can get, from assistants, parents, student teachers, other available adults, or students from upper elementary classes.
4. Don't be too ambitious. Less on a regular basis is better than more inconsistently.
5. Central office personnel, not classroom teachers, should assemble Level Three, the quantified data, although teachers should be consulted to check for accuracy.

PRINCIPLES OF EVALUATION

The following principles, which are consistent with developmental theory, inform the procedures suggested in this chapter.

1. To be significant, evaluation of literacy learning should be concerned with real, not contrived, activities; real reading and writing rather than skills testing.
2. Description should be primary and provide the basis for interpretation and evaluation.
3. Evaluation of a developmental process like literacy learning should itself be developmental, that is, longitudinal.
4. The primary function of evaluation is to inform teaching.
5. Evaluation should be supportive of learning.
6. Evaluation should recognize the individual character of the learner—allowing differences in both styles and rates of learning.

Finally, evaluation that dampens children's natural desire to participate in the surrounding culture and that discriminates or labels cannot be justified in any terms: not in the name of policy setting or accountability. To see high standardized test scores as an educational goal is surely to live in an Alice-in-Wonderland world—where, ultimately, no one except politicians gets anywhere. The game may be making political vulnerable education *look good,* but we cannot allow it to be played when it results in making young children *feel bad.* The determining criterion of good literacy evaluation can be direct and sensible: whether both process and results bring each child greater access to the pleasures and benefits of reading and writing.

CHAPTER NOTES AND REFERENCES

Chapter 2. Literacy Acquisition and the Representation of Language, pp. 31–55.

References

Blanche-Benveniste, C., and Chervel, A. *L'orthographe.* Paris: Maspero, 1974.

Cohen, M. *La grande invention de l'écriture et son évolution.* Paris: Klincksieck, 1958.

Ferreiro, E. "The Underlying Logic of Literacy Development." In *Awakening to Literacy,* edited by H. Goelmann, A. Oberg, and F. Smith. Portsmouth, N.H.: Heinemann, 1984a.

_____. *La práctica del dictado en el primer año escolar.* Mexico: Cuadernos de Investigacion DIE No. 15, 1984b.

_____. "Literacy Development: A Psychogenetic Perspective." In *Literacy, Language and Learning,* edited by D. Olson, N. Torrance, and A. Hildyard. New York: Cambridge University Press, 1985.

_____. "The Interplay Between Information and Assimilation in Beginning Literacy." In *Emergent Literacy,* edited by W. Teale and E. Sulzby. Norwood, N.J.: Ablex, 1986.

Ferreiro, E., and Gómez Palacio, M., eds. *Nuevas perspectivas sobre los procesos de lectura y escritura.* Mexico: Siglo XXI Editores, 1982.

Ferreiro, E., and Teberosky, A. *Literacy Before Schooling.* Portsmouth, N.H.: Heinemann, 1982. (Original work published 1979)

Freeman, Y., and Whitesell, L. "What Preschoolers Already Know About Print." *Educational Horizons* 64 (1985): 22-24.

Gelb, I. *A Study of Writing.* Chicago: University of Chicago Press, 1952. (Original work published 1976)

Piaget, J. *The Equilibration of Cognitive Structures.* Chicago: University of Chicago Press, 1985. (Original work published 1975)

Saussure, F. de. *Course in General Linguistics.* New York: McGraw-Hill, 1966. (Original work published 1915)

Teberosky, A. "Construcción de escritura a través de la interacción grupal." In *Nuevas perspectivas sobre los procesos de lectura y escritura*, edited by E. Ferreiro and M. Gómez Palacio. Mexico: Siglo XXI Editores, 1982.

Notes

1. I shall confine my discussion to the alphabetical writing system.
2. The population of a city or its political significance may also be represented, for example, by different forms (i.e., squares or circles) or by different sizes of the same form. In this case, the analogic relationship is restored within an arbitrary relationship.
3. "Spontaneous writing productions" are those that are not the result of a copy (either immediate or deferred). I shall confine my discussion to the processes involved in the production of texts (writing) and shall not go into the processes involved in the interpretation of texts (reading), though both are closely related (which does not mean that they run in parallel).
4. The key phrase here is *a set of words.* Isolated writing attempts are generally impossible to interpret. The task of assessing the contrasts that are taken into account in the construction of the representations can be done properly only within a set of written words.
5. All the illustrations belong to children of very poor urban sectors attending kindergarten or primary school in Mexico City.
6. For a fuller explanation of the transition from conceiving letters as objects to conceiving them as substitute objects, see Ferreiro 1984a.
7. Similar data have been reported with English-speaking children by Freeman and Whitesell 1985.
8. Kamii, Long, Manning, and Manning (Chapter 4 of this volume) as well as other authors have reported English examples of syllabic writing that have in common that consonants are more frequent than vowels (for instance, SPM for *superman,* VKN for *vacation).* In spite of this difference, it seems misleading to speak about a *consonantal* level instead of syllabic level. In fact, English- as well as Spanish-speaking children choose one letter for a part of a word that corresponds to more than one phoneme. Spanish-speaking children prefer to use vowels (but consonants are not excluded); English-speaking children prefer to use consonants (but vowels are not excluded). Both seem to be influenced by the peculiar

characteristics of their native language. More research of a truly comparative nature is needed to clarify these issues.

9. I am using here Piaget's 1975/1985 model of equilibration.

10. A study of one of these practices, namely dictation, may be found in Ferreiro 1984b.

11. It is for this reason that the term "lecto-escritura" ("reading-writing") has been coined.

12. In several earlier publications, I have emphasized that nothing can be defined, in absolute terms, as "easy" or "difficult." Something is easy when it corresponds to the assimilatory schemes available and difficult when the schemes have to be modified. For this reason, there are things that may be easy at one moment in time and difficult at another. For example, the recognition of a given letter as the initial of a proper name is easy when it is interpreted as "mine" or "my sister's letter." However, when it comes to the construction of the syllabic hypothesis and this initial is given the value of the first syllable of a name, new problems arise: For example, a child called Ramon interprets the first letter of his name (R) as "ra" and finds it difficult to understand why his friend Rosa, who has the same initial, says that R stands for "ro."

13. This is an advertisement for foreign language courses which was circulating in Europe a few years ago.

14. This applies to the majority of schools. There are, of course, some projects, in the United States and Latin America, that apply similar principles as those indicated in this [chapter].

15. This goes against the well-spread notion that the teacher could become "the scribe of the class" because, by doing this, s/he continues to be the only one who can write in the classroom.

16. In a discussion on this theme, Hermine Sinclair used a most suitable expression to warn us of the dangers involved in the notion of reading readiness: "One of the things that I have tried to say in this conference is that we are not (scientifically) prepared to talk about reading readiness, and until we are it would be better to assume that every child in the classroom is ready to read than to assume that we can classify those who do not have what we assume that we know that they ought to have" (cited in Ferreiro and Gómez Palacio, eds., 1982, p. 349).

Chapter 3. Principles of Spelling Found in the First Two Grades, pp. 57–68.

References

Anis, J. *L'écriture, théories et description.* Bruxelles: De Boeck Université, 1988.

Berthoud-Papandropoulou, I. "An Experimental Study of Children's Ideas About Language." In *The Child's Conception of Language,* edited by A. Sinclair, R. J. Jarvella, and W. J. M. Lendt. Berlin, Heidelberg, and New York: Springer-Verlag, 1978.

Blanche-Benveniste, C., and Chervel, A. *L'orthographe.* Paris: Maspero, 1969.

Bloomfield, L. *Language.* London: Allen and Unwin, 1933.

Catach, N. *L'orthographe.* Paris: Presses Universitaires de France, 1978.

Derrida, J. *Of Grammatology.* Baltimore: Johns Hopkins University Press, 1976.

Ferreiro, E., and Teberosky, A. *Literacy Before Schooling.* Portsmouth, N.H.: Heinemann, 1982.

Kamii, C. *Young Children Reinvent Arithmetic.* New York: Teachers College Press, 1985.

_____. *Young Children Continue to Reinvent Arithmetic—2nd Grade.* New York: Teachers College Press, 1989.

Lyons, J. *Language and Linguistics.* Cambridge: Cambridge University Press, 1981.

Sampson, G. *Writing Systems.* London, Hutchinson and Stanford: Stanford University Press, 1985.

Siegrist, F. "La conceptualisation du système alphabétique et orthographique du français par l'enfant de 6 à 9 ans." Ph.D. diss., University of Geneva, 1986.

_____. "Acquisition de l'orthographe et correspondence phonographique." *Bulletin d'audiophonologie,* in press.

Chapter 4. Spelling in Kindergarten: A Constructivist Analysis Comparing Spanish-Speaking and English-Speaking Children, pp. 69–82.

References

Bissex, G. *GYNS AT WRK: A Child Learns to Write and Read.* Cambridge, Mass.: Harvard Unviversity Press, 1980.

Chomsky, C. "Approaching Reading Through Invented Spelling." In *Theory and Practice of Early Reading.* Vol. 2., edited by L. B. Resnick and P. A. Weaver, 43–65.Hillsdale, N.J.: Erlbaum, 1979.

Ferreiro, E., and GómezPalacio, M. *Análisis de las perturbaciones en el preceso de aprendizaje de la lecto-escritura.* Mexico City: Dirección General de EducatiónEspecial, 1982.

Ferreiro, E., and Teberosky, A. *Literacy Before Schooling.* Portsmouth, N.H.: Heinemann, 1982.

Henderson, E. H. *Learning to Read and Spell: The Child's Knowledge of Words.* DeKalb, Ill.: Northern Illinois University Press, 1981.

Piaget, J. *The Child's Conception of the World.* Totowa, N.J.: Littlefield, Adams and Co, 1967.

Read, C. *Children's Categorization of Speech Sounds in English.* Urbana, Ill.: National Council of Teachers of English, 1975.

Chapter 6. Shared Book Experience: Teaching Reading Using Favorite Books, pp. 91–109.

References

Ashton-Warner, S. *Teacher.* New York: Simon and Schuster, 1963.

Aulls, M. W. *Developing Readers in Today's Elementary School.* Boston: Allyn and Bacon, 1982.

Barrett, F. L. *A Teacher's Guide to Shared Reading.* Toronto: Scholastic, 1982.

Bennett, J. *Learning to Read with Picture Books.* Gloucester, Ont.: Thimble Press, 1979.

Butler, D. *Cushia and Her Books.* Auckland: Hodder and Stoughton, 1979.

_____. *Babies Need Books.* Toronto: Bodley Head, 1980.

Butler, D, and Clay, M. *Reading Begins at Home.* Auckland: Heinemann, 1979.

Clay, M. *Reading: The Patterning of Complex Behavior.* Auckland: Heinemann, 1972.

_____. *The Early Detection of Reading Difficulties: A Diagnostic Survey with Recovery Procedures.* Auckland: Heinemann, 1980.

Eastman, P. D. *Are You My Mother?* New York: Beginner Books, 1960.

Goodman, K. S., ed. *The Psycholinguistic Nature of the Reading Process.* Detroit: Wayne State University Press, 1968.

Goodman, K., and Goodman, Y. M. "Learning to Read Is Natural." In *Theory and Practice of Early Reading,* Vol. 1, edited by L. B. Resnick and P. B. Weaver, 137–54. Hillsdale, N.J.: Lawrence Erlbaum Associates, 1979.

Goodman, Y. M. and Burke, C. *Reading Strategies: Focus on Comprehension.* New York: Holt Rinehart, 1980.

Holdaway, D. *The Foundations of Literacy.* Sydney: Ashton Scholastic, 1979.

Horton, J. *On the Way to Reading.* Wellington: Department of Education, 1978.

McCracken, M. J., and Robert A. *Reading, Writing and Language,* Winnipeg: Pegius Publishers, 1979.

Martin, Jr., B. and Brogan, P. *Teacher's Guide to the Instant Readers.* New York: Holt, Rinehart and Winston, 1982.

Meek, M. *Learning to Read.* London: Bodley Head, 1982.

Pulvertaft, A. *Carry on Reading.* Sydney: Ashton Scholastic, 1978.

Smith, F. *Understanding Reading,* 2d ed. New York: Holt, Rinehart and Winston, 1978.

Temple, C. A.; Nathan, R. G.; and Burris, N. *The Beginnings of Writing.* Boston: Allyn and Bacon, 1982.

Veatch, J. *Individualizing Your Reading Program.* New York: Putnam, 1959.

Children's Books

Greenfield, E. *Grandmama's Joy*. Illust. by Carol Byard. New York: Philomel Books, 1980.

Grosvenor, D. K. *The Blue Whale*. Illus. by Larry Foster. Washington, D.C.: National Geographic Society, 1977.

Hoberman, M. A. *A House Is a House for Me*. Illus. by Betty Fraser. New York: Viking Press, 1978.

Spier, P. *People*. Garden City, N.Y.: Doubleday, 1980.

GENERAL REFERENCES

Altwerger, B.; Edelsky, C.; and Flores, B. "Whole Language: What's New?" *The Reading Teacher* 41 (1987): 144-54.

Anis, J. *L'écriture, théories et description*. Bruxelles: De Boeck Université, 1988.

Ashton-Warner, S. *Teacher*. New York: Simon and Schuster, 1963.

Aulls, M. W. *Developing Readers in Today's Elementary School*. Boston: Allyn and Bacon, 1982.

Barrett, F. L. *A Teacher's Guide to Shared Reading*. Toronto: Scholastic, 1982.

Bennett, J. *Learning to Read with Picture Books*. Gloucester, Ontario: Thimble Press, 1979.

Berthoud-Papandropoulou, I. "An Experimental Study of Children's Ideas About Language." In *The Child's Conception of Language*, edited by A. Sinclair, R. J. Jarvella, and W. J. M. Lendt. Berlin, Heidelberg, and New York: Springer-Verlag, 1978.

Bissex, G. *GYNS at WRK: A Child Learns to Read and Write*. Cambridge, Mass.: Harvard University Press, 1980.

Blanche-Benveniste, C., and Chervel, A. *L'orthographe*. Paris: Maspero, 1969.

Bloomfield, L. *Language*. London: Allen and Unwin, 1933.

Butler, D. *Babies Need Books*. Toronto: Bodley Head, 1980.

Butler, D., and Clay, M. *Reading Begins at Home*. Auckland: Heinemann, 1979.

Catach, N. *L'orthographe*. Paris: Universitaires de France, 1978.

Chomsky, C. "Approaching Reading Through Invented Spelling." In *Theory and Practice of Early Reading*, Vol. 2, edited by L. B. Resnick and P. A. Weaver, 43-65. Hillsdale, N.J.: Erlbaum, 1979.

Clay, M. *Reading: The Patterning of Complex Behaviors*. Auckland: Heinemann, 1972.

_____. *The Early Detection of Reading Difficulties: A Diagnostic Survey with Recovery Procedures*. Auckland: Heinemann, 1980.

Clements, D. H., and Battista, M. T. "Constructivist Learning and Teaching." *Arithmetic Teacher*, 38 (1990): 34-35.

Cohen, M. *La grande invention de l'écriture et son évolution*. Paris: Klincksieck, 1958.

Derrida, J. *Of Grammatology*. Baltimore: Johns Hopkins University Press, 1976.

Duckworth, E.; Easley, J.; Hawkins, D.; and Henriques, A. *Science Education: A Minds-On Approach for the Elementary Years*. Hillsdale, N.J.: Erlbaum, 1990.

Eberhart, S.; Philhower, R.; Sabatino, M.; Smith, D., and Waterhouse, R. "Taking Misconceptions into Account Can Throw New Light on Shadows." *Power Line* l, no. 1 (1990): l-5.

Ferreiro, E. "The Underlying Logic of Literacy Development." In *Awakening to Literacy*, edited by H. Goelmann, A. Oberg, and F. Smith. Portsmouth, N.H.: Heinemann, 1984a.

_____. *La práctica del dictado en el primer año escolar*. Mexico: Cuadernos de Investigacion DIE No. l5., 1984b.

_____. "Literacy Development: A Psychogenetic Perspective." In *Literacy, Language and Learning*, edited by D. Olson, N. Torrance, and

A. Hildyard, 217-28. New York: Cambridge University Press, 1985.

____. "The Interplay Between Information and Assimilation in Beginning Literacy." In *Emergent Literacy*, edited by W. Teale and E. Sulzby, 15-49. Norwood, N.J.: Ablex, 1986.

Ferreiro, E., and Gómez Palacio, M. *Análisis de la perturbaciones en el proceso de aprendizaje de la lecto-escritura (Analysis of disturbances in the process of learning reading-writing)*. Mexico City: Dirección General de Educación Especial, 1982.

____., eds. *Nuevas perspectivas sobre los procesos de lectura y escritura*. Mexico: Siglo XXI Editores, 1982.

Ferreiro, E., and Teberosky, A. *Literacy Before Schooling*. Exeter, N.H.: Heinemann, 1982.

Fosnot, C. T. *Enquiring Teachers, Enquiring Learners: A Constructivist Approach for Teaching*. New York: Teachers College Press, 1989.

Freeman, Y., and Whitesell, L. "What Preschoolers Already Know About Print." *Educational Horizons* 64 (1985): 22-24.

Furth, H. G. *Piaget and Knowledge*. Englewood Cliffs, N.J.: Prentice-Hall, 1969.

Gelb, I. *A Study of Writing*. Chicago: University of Chicago Press, 1952.

Goodman, K. "Miscues: Windows on the Reading Process." In *Miscue Analysis: Applications to Reading Instruction*, edited by K. Goodman, 5. Urbana, Ill.: National Council of Teachers of English, 1979.

____. *What's Whole in Whole Language?* Portsmouth, N.H.: Heinemann, 1986.

Goodman, K. S., ed. *The Psycholinguistic Nature of the Reading Process*. Detroit: Wayne State University Press, 1968.

Goodman, K., and Goodman, Y. "Learning to Read Is Natural." In *Theory and Practice of Early Reading*, Vol. l, edited by L. B. Resnick and R. B. Weaver, 37-54. Hillsdale, N.J.: Erlbaum, 1979.

Goodman, Y. "Roots of the Whole-Language Movement." *The Elementary School Journal* 90 (1989): 114-27.

Goodman, Y., ed. *How Children Construct Literacy*. Newark, Del.:

International Reading Association, 1990.

Goodman, Y. M., and Burke, C. *Reading Strategies: Focus on Comprehension.* New York: Holt Rinehart, 1980.

Graves, D. *Writing: Teachers and Children at Work.* Exeter, N.H.: Heinemann, 1983.

Henderson, E. H. *Learning to Read and Spell: The Child's Knowledge of Words.* Dekalb, Ill.: Northern Illinois University, 1981.

Holdaway, D. *The Foundations of Literacy.* Sydney: Ashton Scholastic, 1979.

Horton, J. *On the Way to Reading.* Wellington, N.Z.: Department of Education, 1978.

Inhelder, B., and Piaget, J. *The Early Growth of Logic in the Child.* New York: Harper and Row, 1964.

Kamii, C. *Number in Preschool and Kindergarten.* Washington, D.C.: National Association for the Education of Young Children, 1982.

_____. *Young Children Reinvent Arithmetic.* New York: Teachers College Press, 1985.

_____. *Young Children Continue to Reinvent Arithmetic, 2nd Grade.* New York: Teachers College Press, 1989.

Labinowicz, E. *Learning from Children: New Beginnings for Teaching Numerical Thinking.* Menlo Park, Calif: Addison-Wesley, 1985.

Lyons, J. *Language and Linguistics.* Cambridge: Cambridge University Press, 1981.

McCracken, M. J., and McCracken, R. A. *Reading, Writing, and Language.* Winnipeg: Peguis Publishers, 1979.

Martin Jr., B., and Brogan, P. *Teacher's Guide to the Instant Readers.* New York: Holt, Rinehart and Winston, 1972.

Meek, M. *Learning to Read.* London: Bodley Head, 1982.

Piaget, J. *Judgment and Reasoning in the Child.* Paterson, N.J.: Littlefield, Adams and Co, 1964.

_____. *The Child's Conception of Physical Causality.* Paterson, N.J.: Littlefield, Adams and Co., 1966.

_____. *The Child's Conception of the World.* Paterson, N.J.: Littlefield, Adams and Co., 1967.

_____. *The Child's Conception of Time.* New York: Ballantine, 1976.

_____. "The Development in Children of the Idea of the Homeland and of Relations with Other Countries." In *Piaget Sampler,* edited by S. F. Campbell. New York: Wiley, 1976.

_____. *The Equilibration of Cognitive Structures.* Chicago: University of Chicago Press, 1985.

Piaget, J., and Garcia, R. *Psychogenesis and the History of Science.* New York: Columbia University Press, 1989.

Pulvertaft, A. *Carry on Reading.* Sydney: Ashton Scholastic, 1978.

Read, C. "Children's Categorization of Speech Sounds." NCTE Research Report No. l7. Urbana, Ill,: National Council of Teachers of English, 1975.

Sampson, G. *Writing Systems.* London: Hutchinson and Stanford and Stanford University Press, 1985.

Saussure, F. de. *Course in General Linguistics.* New York: McGraw-Hill, 1966.

Siegrist, F. "La conceptualisation du système alphabétique et orthographique du français par l'enfant de 6 à 9 ans." Ph.D. diss., University of Geneva, 1986.

_____. "Acquisition de l'orthographe et correspondance phonographique." *Bulletin d'audiophonologie,* in press.

Smith, F. *Understanding Reading.* 2d ed. New York: Holt, Rinehart and Winston, 1978.

Steffe, L., and Cobb, P. *Construction of Arithmetical Meanings and Strategies.* New York: Springer-Verlag, 1988.

Teale, W., and Sulzby, E. *Emergent Literacy: Writing and Reading.* Norwood, N.J.: Ablex, 1986.

Teberosky, A. "Construcción de escritura a través de la interacción grupal." In *Nuevas perspectivas sobre los procesos de lectura y escritura,* edited by E. Ferreiro and M. Gómez Palacio, 155-78. Mexico: Siglo XXI Editores, 1982.

Temple, C. A.; Nathan, R. G.; and Burris, N. *The Beginnings of Writing*. Boston: Allyn and Bacon, 1982.

Veatch, J. *Individualizing Your Reading Program*. New York: Putnam, 1959.

Watson, B., and Konicek, R. "Teaching for Conceptual Change: Confronting Children's Experience." *Phi Delta Kappan* 71 (1990): 680-85.

Yackel, E.; Cobb, P.; Wood, T.; and Merkel, G. "Experience, Problem Solving, and Discourse as Central Aspects of Constructivism." *Arithmetic Teacher* 38 (1990): 34-35.

CHILDREN'S BOOKS

Butler, D. *Cushla and Her Books*. Auckland: Hodder and Stoughton, 1979.

Eastman, P. D. *Are You My Mother?* New York: Beginner Books, 1960.

Greenfield, E. *Grandmama's Joy*. New York: Philomel Books, 1980.

Grosvenor, D. K. *The Blue Whale*. Washington, D.C.: National Geographic Society, 1977.

Hoberman, M. A. *A House Is a House for Me*. New York: Viking Press, 1978.

Spier, P. *People*. Garden City, N.Y.: Doubleday, 1980.